THE BASICS OF
CORSET BUILDING

A HANDBOOK FOR BEGINNERS
BY LINDA SPARKS

ST. MARTIN'S GRIFFIN ❧ NEW YORK

www.stmartins.com

Illustrations by Vanessa Palmer, Linda Sparks, and Nancy Hastings-Trew
Photographs by Linda Sparks
Layout by hypertext digital publishing
Edited by Janet Dimond

ISBN-13: 978-0-312-53573-5
ISBN-10: 0-312-53573-2

First published in Canada

First U.S. Edition: January 2009

10 9 8 7 6 5 4 3 2 1

Special Thanks to
Tim Sparks for always supporting me.

Dedicated to Vera FitzGerald
and grandmothers everywhere – you have the power to inspire.

THE BASICS OF CORSET BUILDING

Table of Contents

Foreword **1**

Section One
Tools and Materials for Corset Building **3**

   1. Tools 3
   2. Textiles 8
   3. Steel and Plastic 12

Section Two
Building a Corset **19**

   1. Labeling 19
   2. Measuring for Bone Length 20
   3. Working with Plastic Bones 21
   4. Working with Spiral Steel Bones 23
   5. Working with Spring Steel/White Bones 24
   6. Working with an Opening Busk 26
   7. Setting Grommets or Eyelets 30
   8. Applying Lacing Tape and Lacing Bones 32
   9. Applying Lace Tips 36
  10. Lacing a Corset 37
  11. Making and Applying Bias Tape and Petersham Ribbon 40

Section Three
Construction Techniques **45**

   1. Making a Modesty Panel 45
   2. Making a Mock-up 47
   3. Building a Single Layer Corset 48
   4. Building a Double Layer Corset 51
   5. Building a Fashion Fabric Corset 58

Section Four
Pattern Alterations and Fit **63**

   1. Commercial Corset Patterns 63
   2. Fitting a Corset 64
   3. Styling a Corset 72

Glossary **75**

Foreword

This book has been written to explain in illustrated detail the process of building a corset. It was written for those people who have never made a corset but do have basic sewing skills – you can sew a straight line. Sewing a corset isn't quite accurate as the process is more involved than just sewing. You have to know how to work with **tin snips**, **needle-nose pliers** and hammers (not your usual tools for a sewing project), hence the term *building*. This book will introduce you to all of these tools and their application to corset building. The Victorian style corset is used to demonstrate most of our techniques, but that doesn't mean they can only be applied to the corsets of the Victorian period. The techniques outlined here can be applied to corsets of almost any time period, as well as to bridal and evening **bodices** and even men's **doublets.** Consider using what you learn here on any project that requires structure.

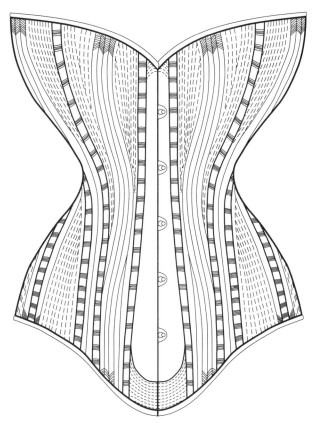

My background is theatre and this means I look for quick and efficient ways to make durable long-wearing garments. This book doesn't discuss couturier methods you can easily implement the techniques. Once you have the basic understanding of how a corset is put together, you can easily include your own finishing style, appliqués, and design details to create your own signature style corset. This book is just the beginning!

Commercial corset patterns by Laughing Moon and Simplicity are used for all of our samples in this book. You should be able to find these patterns easily. I strongly recommend using either the Laughing Moon (Dore) or Simplicity (9769) corset patterns for your first corset as both are excellent patterns and, since they're both discussed here, you'll have all the information you need for a successful project. They also both lend themselves well to fitting and styling.

There is always more than one way to do anything and this book will describe only a few ways to build a corset – but that doesn't mean there are no other ways. You may incorporate construction methods you've learned previously, combine steps from each of these three methods, or have a totally different approach. These methods are described to give you a starting point and a basic understanding of how to build your first corset. Once you've built one I hope you'll be inspired to experiment with other materials and techniques. You don't need a lot of sewing experience to build a corset, but you do need patience, organizational ability, puzzle-solving skills – and the ability to sew a straight line is a huge asset.

A corset isn't a difficult garment to sew, but it's a challenge to build as there are so many pieces and so much hardware. Approach your first corset with time, patience, and an understanding that it won't be a "make it today, wear it tonight" project.

Note: All terms in **bold** are explained for you in the Glossary. And always read *all* the instructions step by step the *first* time.

– Linda Sparks

Corset Map

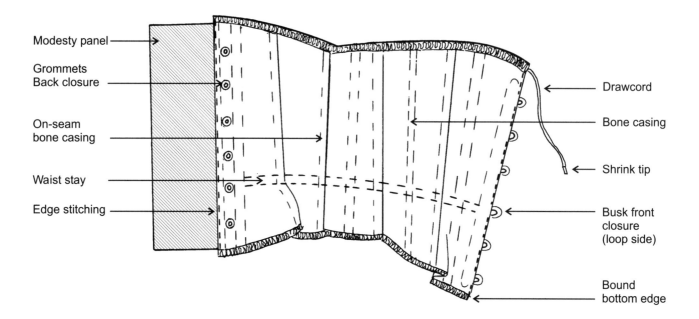

Modesty panel

Grommets
Back closure

On-seam
bone casing

Waist stay

Edge stitching

Drawcord

Bone casing

Shrink tip

Busk front
closure
(loop side)

Bound
bottom edge

A corset has several components and some of these won't be familiar to you. All of the corset building techniques outlined in this book will refer to these parts and you can refer to this illustration as your corset map. This illustration indicates "what is what" and "what goes where." Not all corscts will bc composed of all of the parts shown here but every corset will include some of these elements. All parts labeled on the corset map will be described in depth in other chapters within this book.

Section One: Tools and Materials for Corset Building

1. Tools

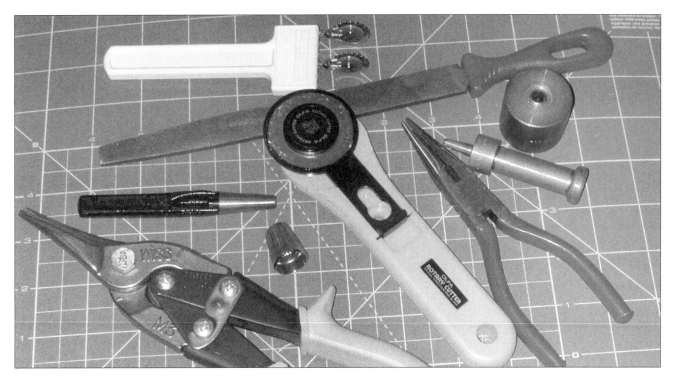

Our discussion won't include machines, only hand-held tools. How many tools you have in your sewing kit will depend on what you sew most often. Most of us have **thimbles**, various **hand-sewing needles**, measuring tape, **tracing wheels**, **thread snips** and scissors – the basics. To build a corset you need all of these and a bit more. For those of you who are new to sewing we'll start with the basic tools listed above, then expand upon them and add a few new ones. Details on exactly how the tools are used will be found in other chapters. This list is to give you an idea of what tools you may need to acquire.

Thimble

Everyone knows what one looks like but it's surprising how many people don't know how or when to use one.

Why should you use a thimble? Because you can't sew efficiently without one and doing so can be dangerous; particularly when sewing heavy fabric that may be difficult to get a needle through.

The thimble protects the middle finger of your sewing hand and gives you more power to push the needle through the fabric. Proper sewing technique requires that you enter the needle into the fabric while holding the needle between forefinger and thumb (A) and then follow through by pushing the needle through the fabric using your middle finger (B). The head of the needle can be very fine and even thicker needles can still puncture your finger before they go through all layers of fabric – if you don't use a thimble for protection. Puncturing your finger will be painful, but worse; it will cause you to bleed and that means you'll get blood on the corset.

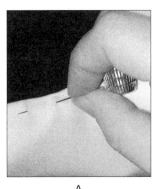

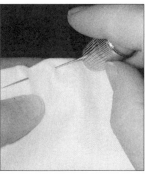

A   B

If you do happen to prick your finger and get blood on the garment, there is a very easy solution.

Blood is inclined to leave a permanent stain unless you use your saliva to dissolve it. Yes, it's true – your saliva will remove the bloodstain – but not if you try this after trying any other options. And only your saliva will dissolve your bloodstain so no one can help you with this. Simply spitting on the garment looks a bit vulgar, so take a yard or meter of thread, ball it up and chew it for a moment, let it get saturated, and then dab the stain with the saturated balled-up wad of thread and watch the bloodstain disappear. If you find this hard to believe, try it.

Hand-sewing Needles

They aren't what they used to be, which is one reason goggles are now part of many sewing rooms. Today's sewing needles tend to be brittle and can snap. Needles come in many sizes. Some sewing specialists will have clear ideas as to which sewing needle to use for which process. I am inclined to say, "Use the needle that feels comfortable to hold." Very large ones aren't practical but a #6 or #7 seems to be reasonable for many purposes. You need hand-sewing needles so that you can finish the top and bottom edges of your corset by hand.

Measuring Tools

A measuring tape is for measuring the body and for checking measurements of the corset. A see-through ruler is my preferred tool for working on patterns and corsets because it not only offers a measuring device but a straightedge as well. I find I need both when corset making. Measuring can be more exact when using a ruler you can see through, and this makes the tracing of straight bone **casing** channels a lot faster. Nothing is better to aid you in marking **bias strips** on fabric than a see-through ruler! And bias strips are needed to finish a corset.

Tracing Wheel

The tracing wheel makes the job of marking all the bone casings much easier, although tailor's tacks can also be used by those who know how to make them. There are several types of tracing wheels: dressmaking, tailor's, and the **double-wheel tracing wheel**. The double-wheel is the most beneficial in corset making. By using it you cut your time in half for marking the casings, and increase your accuracy as the markings can't help but be perfectly parallel. The double-wheel tracing wheel can also be used to mark your **seam allowances**. Align one wheel on your cutting line and the other wheel on the stitching line and you can mark the stitching line perfectly parallel with the cutting line.

Dressmaking tracing wheel

Tailor's tracing wheel

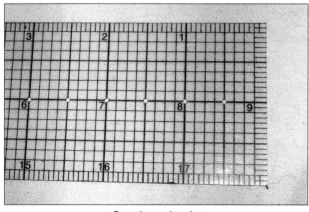

See-through ruler

Double-wheel tracing wheel

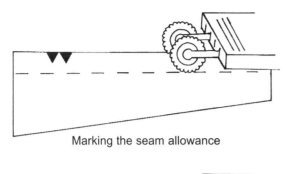

Marking the seam allowance

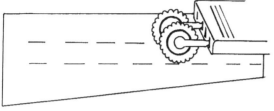

Marking the casing

Thread Snips

Thread snips and scissors are used for cutting out the pattern pieces and snipping the multitude of threads left at the top and bottom of the corset where the bone casing stitching ends. There are a lot of threads since every bone casing requires two rows of stitching. Some Janome sewing machines offer a thread clipping option, but if you don't have one of these high-end machines you'll need to do a lot of clipping by hand. If you're using bone casing ribbon you'll also need to be able to cut the ribbon to length.

Rotary Cutter

A **rotary cutter** isn't absolutely necessary but can make cutting out your pattern pieces easier and saves stress on your hands if you're cutting a lot. To use a rotary cutter you must have a rotary cutting mat to protect your table. Rotary cutters and mats can be purchased at most fabric shops.

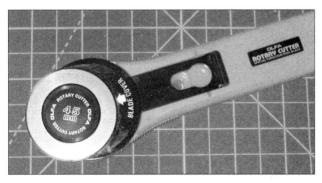

Rotary cutter and mat

Awl

An **awl** is a tool that you won't likely be able to purchase in your local fabric store but you'll find one in almost any hardware store. It's used when you need to apply an opening **busk**. The unique thing about making a hole with an awl is that the threads of the fabric get separated and pushed apart so they don't get cut or broken, and the integrity of the fabric isn't diminished. If you use a hole punch or scissors to create a hole the threads tend to fray and the hole gets bigger; something you want to avoid. This will create a very difficult mending job that will be costly and time consuming.

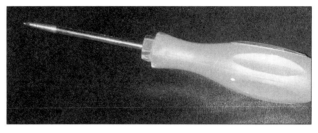

Awl

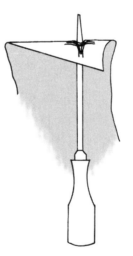

An awl is very simple to use. Simply work the point of the awl between the threads of the fabric where you've marked the hole placement and continue to push the awl through, spreading the threads further and further apart until you have a hole the size you need. Details of this process can be found in Section 2 Chapter 6.

If you can't find an awl, you can use a well-sharpened pencil – but be sure the pencil color is a close match to your fabric as the pencil needs to be very sharp and the lead will be exposed and will mark your fabric.

A hole punch, **rubber mallet**, **bolt cutters**, tin snips, file, and needle-nose pliers are also not likely to be found at your local fabric store, but you may find them in your toolbox. If not, any hardware store should have them.

Earlier we referred to the importance of using an awl rather than cutting a hole to avoid compromising the strength of the fabric. Some people use an awl to form the holes for the grommets or eyelets as well. However this can be a challenging and time-consuming process as there are far more grommets and eyelets than busk knobs, and they tend to be larger than the busk knobs – so grommets are more difficult to force through the awl-made hole. The theory is that by using an awl you won't decrease the strength of the fabric where the grommets/eyelets are set as the threads will remain intact. As a result the grommets will be less inclined to pop out of the fabric. This is true to some extent but using a washer behind the grommet or eyelet increases the security of the grommet or eyelet far more than not cutting a hole would.

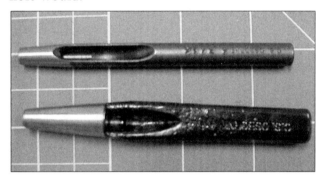

Hole punches

Hole Punches

To make a hole you need a hole punch. Hole punches will come with any grommet or eyelet kit you purchase. It's imperative that the hole you make is the correct size. This will be assured if you use the hole punch that comes with the kit, and then order more grommets or eyelets in the same size as those included in the kit.

Rubber Mallet

Rubber mallets are useful in setting grommets. *Don't use a regular metal hammer,* as the metal hammer striking the metal grommet setter is unsafe. If you can't get a rubber mallet try a rawhide or wooden one. Details on setting grommets or eyelets can be found in Section 2 Chapter 7. There are other means of closing the back of

your corset so if you decide not to use grommets or eyelets then you won't need a rubber mallet. Decide how you'll finish the corset before you buy the tool. See Section 2 Chapter 8 for other options.

Bolt Cutters

Bolt cutters can sometimes be found at dollar stores, but don't waste your money on them. They tend not to do the job, and if they work at first they don't last until the end of the project. The movement of the jaws of a bolt cutter can make it a better cutting tool than tin snips for

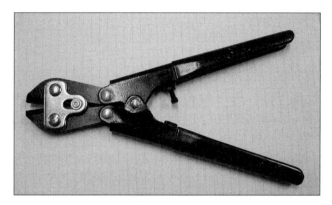

Bolt cutters

some steel. The jaws of a bolt cutter are parallel to one another and clamp down in a way that applies pressure to the whole piece of steel at one time – unlike tin snips which function more like scissors. This means that the steel can't slide out from between the jaws. Bolt cutters are a better choice for **spiral steel bones** and narrower **spring steels**. Details on how to cut steel can be found in Section 2 Chapters 4 and 5.

Tin Snips

Tin snips are another tool for cutting steel bones. Some bones cut more easily with bolt cutters and some with tin snips. Like bolt cutters, tin snips shouldn't be purchased at the dollar or discount store. Regardless of brand name the tin snips should have serrated jaws as they'll grip the steel better and don't allow the steel to slide out from between the jaws. Tin snips function in the same way scissors do, so lack of a serrated jaw means the bone will slide out of the jaws as they close.

Tin snips are best for spring steel, particularly wider spring steels, and for plastic as well.

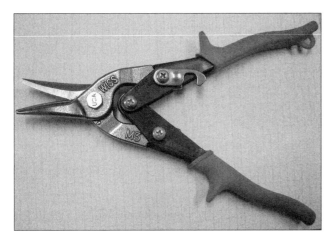

Tin snips

Details on cutting bones and which tools to use for what type of bone can be found in Section 2 Chapters 4 and 5.

File

A file may be needed if you're cutting steel bones. You may need to file off the rough or sharp corners of the steel bones prior to applying **"U" tips**. For cutting and finishing most plastic bones, scissors and an emery board from the drug store will likely be adequate.

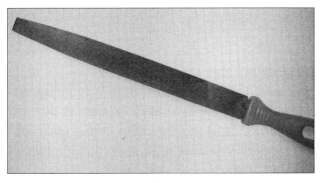

File

Needle-nose Pliers

You'll need to have two pairs of needle-nose pliers if you're cutting steel bones. The cut steel has to be capped with small "U"-shaped ends and the only way to apply these tips is by using two pairs of pliers simultaneously. Full details of this process can be found in Section 2 Chapter 4.

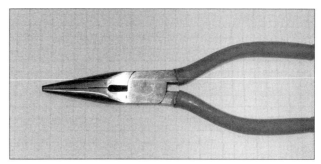

Needle-nose pliers

Goggles

Goggles aren't a tool, but do need to be mentioned. Goggles or protective eye wear should be worn whenever you cut steel or machine stitch the top edge of your corset after sliding the bones into their casings. Cutting spiral steel often results in a little piece flying off and the risk of the machine needle hitting a bone and breaking is high – wear goggles. Wardrobes that abide by health and safety rules will expect you to wear goggles whenever you're at a sewing machine, so you might as well get your own and get accustomed to wearing them.

2. Textiles

There are two types of materials used in corset building: those made of textile fibers and those that aren't. Busks, grommets, and bones are examples of those that aren't made of textile and will be covered later in this section. The next few pages will be dedicated to those materials that are made of textile fibers.

These materials are:
- fabric
- bone casing
- **bias tape** or binding and **petersham**
- **twill tape**
- **cable cord**
- **lacing cord**
- **lacing tips**
- **lacing tape**
- **fusible interfacing.**

Fabric

We're all familiar with fabrics and you can likely identify the difference between satin and denim, but chances are you've never seen **coutil**. Few fabrics have the characteristics of coutil, and few are suitable for the foundation of a corset.

Coutil can be a **brocade,** satin or **herringbone** weave, and cotton or cotton/viscose are the most common fiber contents. Polyester is difficult to work with and doesn't breathe well – it's best avoided.

Coutil's important characteristics are:
- tightly woven
- limited inclination to stretch
- smooth finish
- strength.

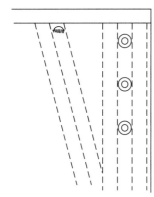

Tightly woven fabric is by nature dense and this is important as bones are less likely to work holes in the fabric. The bones in a corset tend to shift up and down in their casings when the corset is worn, and this shifting can cause holes at the top and bottom of the bone casing – a common problem. This is best dealt with during planning and construction rather than as a repair process because repair is time consuming and rarely attractive. Bone damage to a corset can occur during only one wearing if you don't construct your corset properly. Start with using a tightly woven fabric.

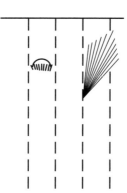

Decorative stitching was traditionally used to help strengthen these areas of wear. This adds a very attractive touch but takes time and more importantly skill.

Stretching of the fabric in a corset defeats the purpose of a corset, however it will still happen to some degree. I've had people suggest denim as an alternative to coutil. But – think about squeezing into a new or freshly washed pair of jeans and then think how they feel at the end of a day. They've stretched. For this reason denim isn't a good choice despite it seeming to be more cost effective. Tightly woven fabric is less inclined to stretch.

A smooth finish is important because the corset is worn tightly and often directly against the skin, and a rough finish can cause unsightly and uncomfortable indentations on your body over the whole area of the corset. So, while some people say they use cotton duck because it doesn't stretch as much as denim does – think twice about doing this to someone you like.

The strength of the fabric you use is extremely important as is the technique for sewing the seams. Remember the corset is snug fitting and you don't want seams bursting or pulling apart. For this reason don't use velvet or satin unless the satin is a coutil. The corset seams will be under a great deal of strain, even if the corset isn't being used to greatly reduce your size.

Note: There are many herringbone twills and those with the smallest herringbone weave are the best, densely woven and with the least inclination to stretch.

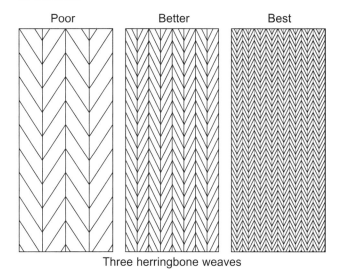

Three herringbone weaves

Coutil has been designed specifically for corset manufacturing, and while it's rather costly it really is the best choice. I know of no comparable fabric.

Bone Casing

Bone casings are used in all corset construction. There are four methods of making bone casings:

- Using two layers of coutil. (A)

- Using the seam allowances. (B)

- Using bone casing ribbon (manufactured for the purpose) and sewn onto the inside of the coutil corset. These ribbon-look bone casings can also be sewn onto the outside of the corset and this can create a design feature, particularly when contrasting color is used. (C)

- Using bone casing ribbon over the seam allowance – this encases any raw edges, creating a beautiful finish as well as holding the bones. (D)

The bone casings must be of a durable woven fabric. If you wish to use satin ribbon as a design feature consider it as an appliqué, applying it over the bone casing. Manufactured bone casing

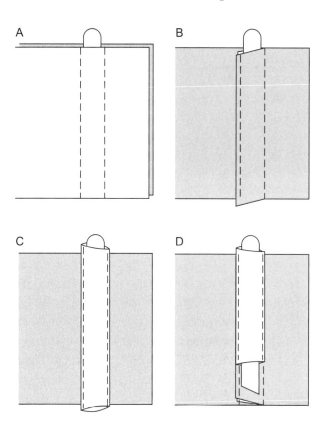

Four types of bone casing

appears to be a basic cotton or rayon ribbon but it's in fact a flattened tube into which you can slide the bone. Bones aren't slid into the casing until after the casing is sewn onto the garment. If you look closely at the manufactured bone casing you'll see the area where you can stitch. Avoid stitching outside this area and into the bone area as you'll have difficulty sliding your bones in later.

Bone casing tape is available in four widths and in two colors only – black and white (and occasionally flesh). Natural fiber content makes bone casing tape easy to dye. Twill tape isn't adequate for bone casing as it's too weak. Prussian tape however is suitable but hard to find. Prussian tape looks much like twill tape but you'll notice a distinct difference in how it feels. It's much more densely woven and stronger, and tends to be made of polyester.

Bias Tape

Bias tape or biais tape – I've seen it spelled both ways but the pronunciation seems to be the same everywhere.

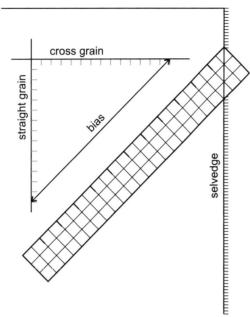

Finding the bias of your fabric

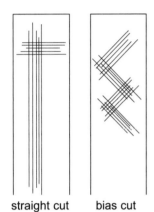

straight cut   bias cut

Bias strips have the ability to bind curved edges without bunching, tucking, or pulling because the **bias** cut allows for subtle stretching and shaping. This can't be accomplished with straight-grain cut goods or most ribbons. Bias tape can be purchased at most fabric stores but making your own in coordinating or contrasting fabric creates a more professional look. Details on this process can be found in Section 2 Chapter 11.

Petersham Ribbon

Some call it grosgrain ribbon and I've heard various theories on the difference between the two. The important details to look for are fiber content and **selvedge**. In binding the edges, petersham ribbon must be able to respond to curves in the same manner as bias tape does – stretching and curving without puckering or pulling. The ribbon's fiber content must be natural; polyester won't allow for the stretching and curving needed. Cotton and cotton/viscose blends work well and can be dyed. The selvedge must not be smooth, but bumpy as the smooth selvedge defines the edge length and won't allow for the

stretch required when binding a curved edge. Petersham ribbon can also be used as the **waist stay** of the corset.

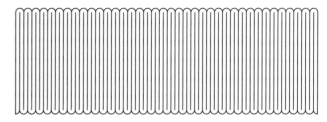

Petersham ribbon — Note the bumpy edge.

Twill Tape

While twill tape isn't adequate for bone casing it's suitable for a waist stay. The twill tape for this should be polyester as it's less inclined to stretch. Twill tape can't be used to bind the top or bottom edge of the corset.

Twill tape

Cable Cord

The reason for a cord at the top of the corset is to gather the top edge very slightly which limits the risk of breasts spilling out. A cord drawing the top edge in makes for a very secure garment for any size woman. Cable cord, fine ribbon or other narrow cord can also be used. This cord should be fairly fine to limit bulk in the bound top edge, and to allow it to be tucked discreetly away to the inside of the corset when the corset is being

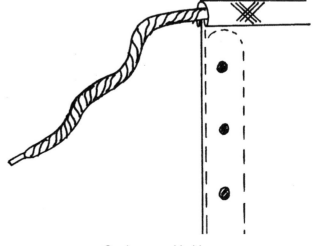

Cord encased in bias

10.

worn. Lace beading can also be used with a ribbon threaded though it. This process makes the draw ribbon both functional and attractive.

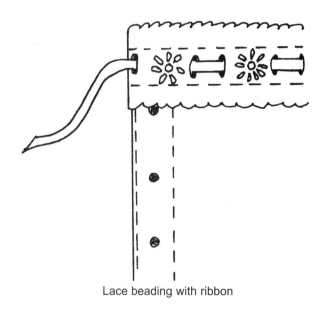

Lace beading with ribbon

Lacing Cord

Usually the lacing cord is found at the center back. Cord fiber content can be of anything, but polyester will be the strongest. Cord should be either knit or braided but not twisted – so don't use cable cord for lacing. The knit cords tend to be flat, and braided cord tends to be round. I prefer the round braided cord as it never appears twisted when laced. Flat cords can twist during the lacing process and while this doesn't affect the strength of the lacing, it can affect the look. Ribbon can also be used but it's harder to work with as it's slippery and the twisting during lacing is very evident and hard to control. It can create a very pretty effect if you have a dresser to help with the lacing, when the look will be worth the time and effort.

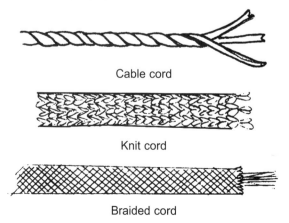

Cable cord

Knit cord

Braided cord

Lacing Tips

Cable cord and lacing cord need to be tipped to keep the ends from fraying and this can be done either with small steel tips called aglets and aglet pliers (which are hard to find and expensive), or with shrink tips. You can also use shoelaces if you can find some that are long enough. More information about tipping laces can be found in Section 2 Chapter 9.

Lacing Tape

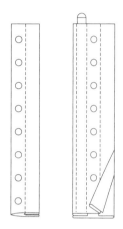

Lacing tape can be sewn to the center back of a corset rather than setting grommets or eyelets. The advantage of lacing tape is that the eyelets have been pre-set by machine so you have no measuring, hole punching, or hammering to set grommets. More information on lacing tape can be found in Section 2 Chapter 8.

Fusible Interfacing

Fusible interfacing isn't an absolute must-have item. A strip of it can be used down the back panel where the grommets are going to be set. Fuse it to the wrong side of the fabric before you punch the holes; it helps keep the fabric around the holes from fraying. This isn't necessary with most coutil but it's a good idea with the fashion fabric layer. Keep the fusible interfacing light to limit the amount of bulk it will add. You may also want to use fusible interfacing on single layer corsets to help increase the bulk if you find the eyelets aren't setting firmly.

3. Steel and Plastic

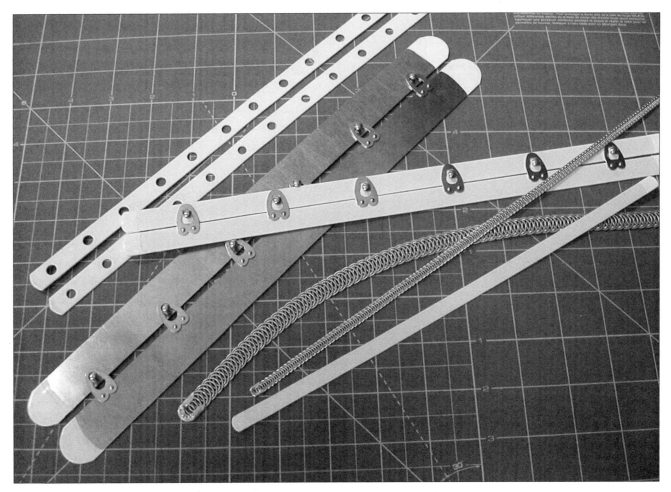

Unlike most garments a corset has several pieces that aren't made from a textile, such as:

- busks
- grommets or eyelets
- grommet or lacing tape
- **lacing bones**
- plastic bones
- steel bones.

Buckles and "D" rings may be found on some corsets as well but we won't be discussing these items as they're not standard.

Busk

A busk today is more than just a strip used for stiffening the front of a corset, and has been since the mid-1800s. Victorian or Edwardian corsets will have an opening busk. The original busks were single pieces that slid into a casing in the center front of a corset and they added stiffer support only – they didn't enable the opening or closing of the corset.

The front opening busk is a two-piece unit that aids the wearer in getting into and out of the corset without assistance as well as adding support. There are two sides to an opening busk, and all opening busks are made of steel. One side is a steel strip with metal loops riveted along one edge, and the other side is a strip of steel with knobs riveted close to one edge that line up with the loops of the other piece. When the two are put together they act much like hook and eye tape. Hook and eye tape can't easily be substituted for a busk as the knobs and loops of a busk are mounted on steel strips, giving both strength and stability. Rarely will a knob or loop come loose as they are riveted to a solid surface. Hooks and eyes are either sewn on or riveted to fabric, and both methods can result in hooks or eyes getting pulled out of the fabric they're anchored to.

The other advantage of a busk is that it doesn't allow any gaping between the hooked points. Think of a blouse that's too snug and how it can gape between the buttons down the center front. This is an impossibility with a busk as the steel foundation can't bend in such a way as to allow gaping. Despite this the busk is flexible enough to be comfortable when you're seated and to allow some bending at the waist. Busks can be purchased in any length from about 6" to 16" but a 12" busk is most commonly used in full-length Victorian and Civil War corsets. As with everything else – all busks are not created equal. You may want to order one straight busk from more than one supplier as there are busks on the market that are easily bent out of shape. Compare them and then decide on your source.

Note: They can look identical but when you flex some they stay bent where others return to straight.

There are three styles of opening busk:

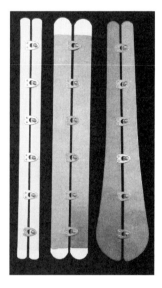

- straight
- wide
- spoon.

The most common and least costly is the straight busk. Each piece is about ½" (13mm) wide and they are white, just like the spring steel bones. They are in fact made of similar materials and are fairly flexible.

Wide busks are stainless steel and silver. Each side is about 1" (25mm) wide and the total width is therefore about 2" (50mm). These offer more substantial support to those women who are large breasted. These are also less flexible than the basic straight busk.

The last and most expensive busk is also made of stainless steel and it's called a spoon busk because it's shaped similar to a spoon. The bowl of the spoon busk fits over the roundness of the stomach and the handle fits upward between the breasts. Spoon busks are historically accurate for a short time period in the late 1800s. They are not commonly used nor mass produced and as a result they're fairly expensive. These are the least flexible busk and in fact tend to be a bit brittle, which makes them a poor choice for **tight lacing**. If you do use one for a tight lacing project, be sure to add support behind them by sliding a bone in behind each side.

More and more runway fashions are featuring corseted evening wear that includes an opening busk. The straight busk is the most common busk for contemporary fashion.

For more information on busks see Section 2 Chapter 6.

Grommets/Eyelets

The terms eyelets and grommets will be used interchangeably throughout this book. Grommets or eyelets with lacing is the best way to close your corset or corset-type bodice as zippers have difficulty withstanding the pressure and are therefore a high-risk closure. If you do choose to use a zipper it needs to be a strong one and should be aided with hooks and eyes. Grommets and eyelets are basically the same thing and serve the same purpose. Grommets tend to have a flatter set and eyelets are a bit more three dimensional. Grommets and eyelets should both be set with washers to decrease the chance of them popping out of the fabric during the lacing process.

Always test set a few grommets or eyelets in the same number of layers of the same fabric as your corset to see how well they set.

Grommets are most commonly made of brass and some are nickel plated – rarely do they come in colors. Eyelets are made of brass, nickel plated or aluminum. Aluminum has the advantage of not corroding when exposed to perspiration. Brass tends to turn green and rough, and nickel plating can cause an allergic reaction to the wearer. I recommend aluminum eyelets for theatrical use to avoid any problems.

The size of grommet you use is a matter of choice. The two most common sizes are #0 – referred to as single aught – with a finished hole diameter of ¼" (6mm), and #00 or double aught with a finished hole diameter of ³/₁₆" (4.7mm).

Note: There is a misperception that the difference between grommets and eyelets is that grommets get set with washers and eyelets don't. This isn't the case; both grommets and eyelets can be set with washers or without. Always include washers in the process when you're corset building.

Lacing Tape

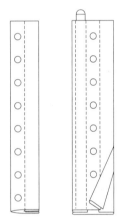

Lacing tape is a fabric tape with grommets/ eyelets already preset on it, and can be sewn to the center back of a corset rather than setting grommets or eyelets. The advantage of lacing tape is that the eyelets have been preset by machine so you have no measuring, hole punching, or hammering to set grommets. This means you don't need the tools required and you don't need to worry about your skill for lining up the eyelets evenly or for setting the eyelets securely. There are two types of lacing tape available and both come in black and white only. The eyelets set in lacing tape don't have washers but are firmly set by machine. For heavy-wear corsets, hand-set grommet or eyelets may be the most secure. You simply sew the lacing tape onto the back of your corset following the instructions in Section 2 Chapter 8.

Lacing Bones

A lacing bone is a rare product and was not found in traditional corsets of any time period – at least not on a regular basis. I've heard of one early 1900s corset that had them but haven't seen nor heard of any other reference to them. The lacing

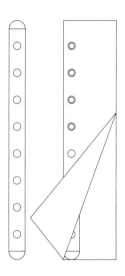

bone gets placed in the center back of the corset. The grommets are essentially set and anchored to the steel, and the fabric is simply a covering and doesn't support the stress on the grommets at all. Despite being strong, the lacing bone should be flexible enough to mould to the natural curve of the back. It isn't visible from the outside of the corset as it's encased in the corset fabric.

More information about lacing bones can be found in Section 2 Chapter 8.

Bones

Bones are also known as **stays** or **steels.** Originally there was whalebone, reeds, or steel that rusted. Today there are three main types of bones and each type can be broken down into sizes and subtypes. These three modern alternatives are:

- plastic – solid and woven
- spiral steel
- spring steel/white bones.

Plastic Boning

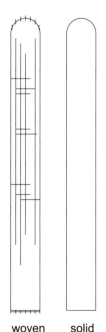

woven   solid

Plastic boning is the simplest form of boning to use. There are a few different types of plastic bones and various trade names as well. Woven plastic boning can be identified easily as it has several rows of fine tubular plastic that are woven together with a fine thread. Woven plastic isn't appropriate for corset building. It's adequate to support a garment but not to support a body. Feather boning is solid plastic boning, and some of these are also not strong enough for corset building. Always test plastic boning before you use it –

does it bend easily and maintain the bent shape rather than returning to being straight? This isn't desirable for corset making. Does it twist when brought near the heat of an iron? Some plastic boning will twist like a corkscrew when brought near steam and this can be a major problem if the corset needs any gentle steaming to remove wear wrinkles.

Plastic Whalebone

This is in theory a replica of the authentic whalebone but it's a distant second. The whalebone I've seen was very fine, very flexible and almost weightless. The plastic whalebone in contrast is dense, thick and much heavier, although still lighter than steel. It can be cut with scissors but can't be sewn through. It's available in three widths and three degrees of thickness: 6mm ($^{15}/_{64}$"), 7mm ($^{9}/_{32}$") and 10mm ($^{25}/_{64}$"). It can be an alternative to spring steel, and depending on which one you use, can be almost as supportive. It's best used in straight lines as it can't curve the way spiral bones or the original whalebone did.

German Plastic Boning

This is the simplest to use. It can be cut with scissors and sewn through which means it can be used many different ways and for a wide variety of projects from corsets to **millinery** or props. Unlike woven plastic bones, once cut there are no prickly ends needing to be dealt with. German plastic boning is available in four widths: 5mm ($^{13}/_{64}$"), 7mm ($^{9}/_{32}$"), 11mm ($^{7}/_{16}$") and 13mm ($^{33}/_{64}$"). It's important to note that all plastic boning can eventually take on the shape of the person's body who is wearing the garment (the more the garment is worn and the hotter the conditions the more likely the plastic is to warp), so while plastic bones create comfortable lightweight garments they may not force the body into a desired shape indefinitely. German plastic bones are the least inclined to mould to the body's shape.

Plastic bones serve their best purpose as an easy way for beginners to learn about boning corsets or in bodices where undergarments will be worn. They're also perfectly acceptable in garments for women who require little support of their breasts and only require support of their garment. A combination of plastic and steel is sometimes a good compromise. Plastic bones can be cut with scissors and the ends blunted by being cut round. Occasionally you may need or want to apply tips to the plastic bones and these are available in only one size. German plastic bones are, in my opinion, the best plastic bones on the market.

Plastic Bone Ends (Tips)

These are a fairly new product and come in one size only. Unlike "U" tips they add length to the bone by about ¾". Take this into consideration if using them. An advantage to these tips is that they can be sewn through and this allows steel to be attached to fabrics. They can also be trimmed to lessen the length, yet still blunt the end.

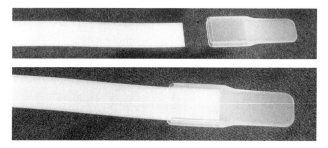

Spiral and Spring Steels

Spiral and spring steels are the most popular bones used by theatres. They can prove a challenge to the first-time corset maker as they require special tools and techniques for cutting and finishing the ends. All steel bones can be purchased in prefinished lengths. To avoid having to cut bones you may want to find out all the available lengths for the style of bone you want, and then draft your corset pattern (or adjust your commercial pattern) to accommodate the bone lengths that you can purchase. Do keep in mind the body you're fitting. Bones that are too long

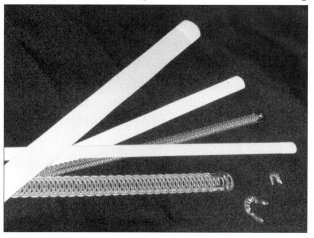

can be very uncomfortable. Fitting information can be found in Section 2 Chapter 2.

Spiral Steels

They're the most flexible of all bones and are less supportive than spring steels and some plastic. Most spirals are grey but do have a protective finish to inhibit rust. This protective finish tends to be oil based and the coils should be wiped down with a rag prior to using them. Some spirals have a white powder coat that makes them a better choice in white garments. This white coating doesn't come off and there are no oil residues on them (they're more costly than the grey ones). The grey spirals are available in two widths, and are sold both in prefinished lengths and by the meter/yard which tends to be the most cost effective (white finished spirals are only sold in prefinished lengths).

Spiral steels are most commonly used in Victorian and Edwardian corsets where many curves need to be followed. They're also the bone of choice for dance costumes as they won't inhibit movement. Cutting these bones requires special tools and the use of "U" tips, which are applied to the cut ends.

Spring Steels

These are typically white as the steel has been coated with a rust-resistant paint. Several widths and a multitude of lengths are available in more than one thickness. The thickness is more important than the width if you're concerned about strength and this goes for both steel and plastic bones. You shouldn't be able to easily bend them – flex yes, but not bend to the point of putting a kink in them. These bones are available in prefinished lengths or by the meter – ready for you to cut to the length you require. This does require special tools. It's important to remember that not all white bones are created equal. They may look the same but always feel them. Consider purchasing just a few bones from various sources to compare them first-hand. Be sure to label them and their source so you can use them for reference later because not all corsets will use the

same bones, and by having a selection you'll be able to make the best choice for your project. More information about working with bones can be found in Section 2 Chapters 2, 3, 4 and 5.

"U" Tips

Even a single wearing can cause holes to develop in the fabric if the steels aren't tipped. The best "U" tips are made of aluminum, making them easy to apply as aluminum is fairly soft. If the tips come off once the bone is encased, not only will the fabric be exposed to the raw edges of the bone, so will the human body! The tip may float around within the casing but this is rarely a problem or a discomfort. The most commonly found are made of steel and are very difficult to apply as they're designed to be put on the ends of bones by machines using thousands of pounds of pressure. Aluminum tips are softer and can be easily identified by squeezing one between your finger and thumb – if it's aluminum you'll be able to crush it. Most steel ones don't have crimping at the base of the "U" but some do, so this isn't a way to identify them. The crimping is important as it helps the "U" tip set smoothly as the crimping takes out the bulk evenly as you squeeze it onto the bone. "U" tips can also be applied to the cut ends of some spring steel/white steel. This technique requires two pairs of pliers and some dexterity.

More information about cutting and tipping spiral bones can be found in Section 2 Chapter 4.

Other Types of Bones

Whalebone was in fact not bone at all but baleen, a long flexible substance found in the mouths of some whales. The sample I saw was dark grey and looked like a bundle of hairs stuck together that could be peeled to make the bone narrower. It was quite flexible in all directions and very light. The spiral steel bones of today are the closest for mobility but much bulkier and heavier. Baleen can't be bought today as it's illegal to trade in whale by-products.

Reeds can be purchased at shops that sell materials for the caning of chairs, and sometimes also at craft stores. Some people resort to using broom straws. This isn't a product I recommend for theatrical use as it's time consuming and the reeds tend to break as they get worn. Once they break they're very difficult to remove from their casing and the broken ends poke through the fabric and into the wearer.

Cording is also an option, but not one I recommend for theatrical use as it's time consuming and doesn't offer the long-term support needed. Cording entails sewing cord into very tight casings. The quality of the cord will affect the support of the corset. Corded corsets can take a very long time to dry when washed! But the advantage is that cord can be sewn in any angle, curve or design.

Most products discussed in this book can be found on-line at **www.farthingales.on.ca**

Section Two: Building a Corset

1. Labeling

One thing that will make the whole construction process easier regardless of which method you choose is labeling your pieces. Labeling is crucial! Corset pattern pieces are not easily recognizable. If you're sewing a blouse and you pick up the sleeve piece, you know it's a sleeve, but corset pieces are very hard to identify as they all look very much alike. It's easy to get pieces sewn on upside down, or in the wrong order. Labeling limits this risk and keeps you from having to think as hard.

Label your pieces in numerical order and be sure to label all of them. Write the number or mark in the seam allowance and keep the placement consistent. I always mark my pieces in the top right and left hand corners within the seam allowances.

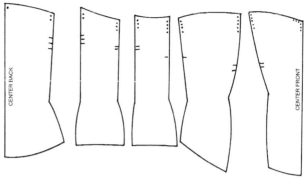

Dot technique for labeling

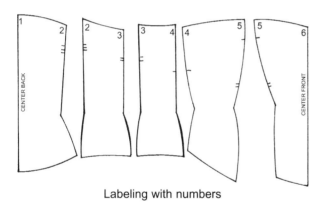

Labeling with numbers

Most pieces have two numbers, one for each side that needs to be sewn to another piece. If you pick up two pieces each with a number 4 in the corner, then you know to match up the corners with the number 4 and stitch those pieces together. It will help to leave your pieces laying on the table in order, and to pick up the first two pieces and sew them together, and then add on the next piece, continuing until each set of panels is done.

If your lining and shell are of the same fabric when making a double layer corset, you may want to use a different labeling technique for each. Maybe use numbers for the shell and a series of dots for the lining. This way you'll avoid inadvertently sewing a lining piece into a shell panel.

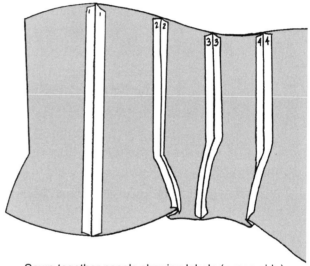

Sewn-together panels showing labels (wrong side)

Note: Shaded areas on illustrations throughout this book indicate wrong side of fabric.

2. Measuring for Bone Length

Regardless of which type of boning you choose you need to determine what lengths you'll need for each casing. This is true whether you're using prefinished lengths of bones or if you're cutting each bone by hand.

Assuming you've already had a fitting or two to determine that the length of your corset is correct for your body, lay your corset mock-up on the table. To find out more about making a mock-up, see Section 3 Chapter 2.

1. Using either a ruler or a measuring tape, measure and mark the stitching line along the top and bottom edges of each corset panel. Be sure to measure every casing because alterations may have affected the symmetry and the two panels may not be identical.

2. Starting at the front measure the length of each casing from the bottom stitching line to the top stitching line.

3. Take this measurement and subtract ½" (13mm) to get the length of bone you need for that casing.

4. Write down the lengths on a sheet of paper in the correct order.

Note: You may want to record the measurements in both metric and imperial (inches) as bones can be sold in either depending on where they were manufactured.

5. Tally the quantity of bones you need in each size. If the bone lengths you need are in-between the bone lengths that are available you can vary the measurement slightly. Bones should be approximately ½" (13mm) shorter than the finished casing but could be as little as a ¼" (6mm) shorter. A ¼" (6mm) is the least amount of difference you should have, and if you go much more than ½" (13mm) the bones can be obviously short.

6. Create a list of the bones you'll need as this will organize the information for either ordering prefinished bones or for cutting bones to size.

Example:

13" (33cm)	x 4
12½" (32cm)	x 6
12" (30.5cm)	x 4
11" (28cm)	x 4

For measuring busk length, please see Section 2 Chapter 6.

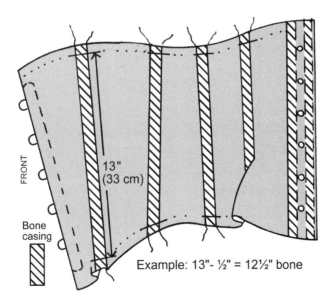

FRONT

13"
(33 cm)

Bone casing

Example: 13"- ½" = 12½" bone

Sewn-together panels with marked stiching lines

3. Working with Plastic Bones

Plastic bones are the simplest bones to work with (provided they're not <u>woven</u> plastic bones).

Woven Plastic Bones

Woven plastic bones, while not really suitable for corset making, may be all you have available. They're readily found in most fabric stores and require no special tools to cut them.

1. Mark the cutting line. Bones should be about ½" (13mm) shorter than the finished casing.
2. Cut the bone with scissors. (A)
3. Finish the end of the bone by either binding the ends with fabric (B) OR melting the ends with a lit candle. (D)
4. Zig-zag stitch over the bone to hold it in place – these bones don't slide well into casings.

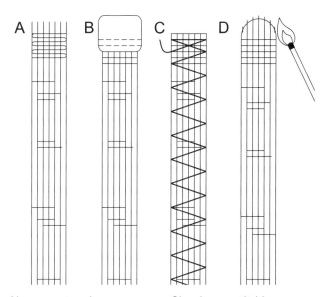

A) raw cut end
B) fabric bound end
C) zig-zag stitching over
D) melted end

Three reasons why I don't recommend these bones:

- The cut ends can be difficult and time consuming to finish. (I don't like the idea of lit candles anywhere near my workspace.)
- Because they don't slide well into casings they have to be sewn in place and this makes them difficult to remove and replace.
- They are usually too light for the job, and once you've gone through all of the above it can be very disappointing and frustrating to have to start over.

Solid Plastic Bones

To work most efficiently you'll want to measure your corset or corset pattern to determine the quantity of each length of bone you'll require. Example: 8 pieces at 12" (30.5cm) and 6 pieces at 12½" (32cm), etc. Once you determine how many bones you need of each length, you can start marking the boning with an indelible marker at the intervals where you'll need to cut the bone lengths. Solid bones can be trimmed to any angle so they can be a good choice for "V"-shaped bodice fronts.

The method of cutting plastic bones is the same regardless of which solid plastic bones you're dealing with.

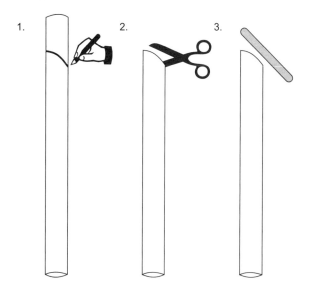

1. Mark cutting lines. Bones should be about ½" (13mm) shorter than the finished casing.
2. Use scissors and cut directly across the bone. If you find cutting the plastic bones with scissors too difficult consider trying tin snips. Shape the cut ends using the scissors. The ends can be rounded or slanted, your choice.
3. Any rough spots can be filed off with an emery board or nail file.

No tipping or finishing is required, however "U" tips can be used if sizes are appropriate.

Note: If the plastic boning has been stored as a coil the boning will be inclined to maintain the curved shape. To avoid this affecting your garment you should do one of two things:

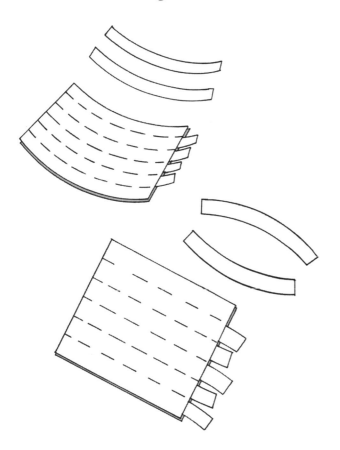

moves through the knob. The ticking sound indicates that the tie is locking into place and can't come undone. These ties come in many lengths and a few different widths – the bigger the better for corset making. They can be an economical substitute if bought in bulk but can rarely be found in lengths more than 14" (12.8cm). Considering the waste they've been known to end up costing more than plastic bones by the meter/yard. These "bones" can be cut with scissors, require no finishing of the ends, and can slide easily into a casing. They're quite flexible and some are comparable to some plastic bones on the market. Be sure to purchase white ones; they do come in other colors but dark colors will show through light fabrics. And don't forget to cut off the knob end!

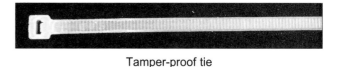

Tamper-proof tie

After you've cut your pieces you may want to soak them in warm water (they're plastic so this won't cause any problems), then work them with your hands pulling them and straightening them, working to curve them in the opposite direction of the curve they already have.

OR

When you slide them into their casings alternate the direction in which they curve. If the first bone is concaved and curves into the body then slide the next bone in so that it's convex and curves away from the body. If you insert all the bones so they curve in the same direction you'll end up with a warped garment that looks somewhat like a strip of spareribs! By alternating the direction of the curve you'll have the bones working against each other's curve and they'll be more inclined to straighten out.

Tamper-proof Ties

While tamper-proof ties (a.k.a. "zip" ties) aren't technically bones, they can be used in a pinch for some corsets. A tamper-proof tie isn't a twist tie. They're usually white plastic but can come in other colors. They have a rectangular knob at one end, and the opposite flat end gets threaded through this knob, producing a ticking sound as it

4. Working with Spiral Steel Bones

To work most efficiently you'll want to measure your corset or corset pattern to determine the quantity of each length of bone you'll require. Example: 8 pieces at 12" (30.5cm) and 6 pieces at 12½" (32cm), etc. Once you determine how many bones you need of each length, you can start marking the boning with an indelible marker at the intervals where you'll need to cut the bone lengths.

Cutting Spiral Bones

Note: You'll need to use bolt cutters.

1. Mark the cutting line. Bones should be about ½" (13mm) shorter than the finished casing.

2. Using bolt cutters, align the cutting mark on the outside wire of the spiral bone with the tip of the bolt cutter jaws. Snip the outer wire only.

3. Flip the bone over and do the same on the other side.

4. The bone should come apart in two pieces.

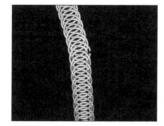
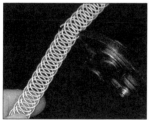
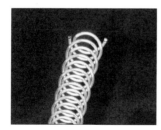

If the bone doesn't come apart:

5. Bend the bone at the crease created by the cutting attempt and the bone will break at these points. You may have to snip it again. Don't try to cut through the whole bone as it results in a messy cut and can be more difficult to tip. It also takes more effort and if you have many bones to cut you'll want to save your hands whenever possible.

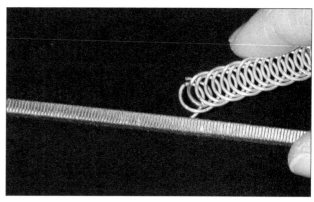

6. The cut wires shouldn't be protruding, so clip the raw end again to shorten or file using the small file:

   a) Place the file flat on the table.

   b) Hold the file still with one hand and drag the wire across it, toward you, then repeat until the wire isn't protruding beyond the width of the bone.

Finishing Spiral Bones – (Applying Tips)

Note: You'll need two pairs of needle-nose pliers.

"U" tips were designed for spiral bones and they're the best way to finish the ends.

Attaching the "U" tips is a bit complicated and takes some practise. Have all your bones cut to size, and then have them and the tips within easy reach.

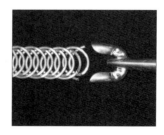
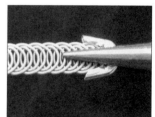
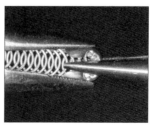
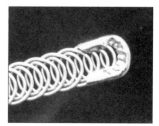

1. Place one pair of needle-nose pliers in your right hand. Place one tip, flat, between the jaws. Gently apply pressure so that you're gripping the tip but not squishing it.

2. Pick up a bone, slide the cut end into the tip, squeeze the pliers a bit to grip the tip and the bone.

3. Pick up the second set of pliers in your left hand, apply the jaws to either side of the tip. Apply pressure to both sets of pliers simultaneously.

If you apply pressure in only one direction the tip pops out in the opposite direction. Some people say they resort to glue to help – if you do this, use the glue sparingly. There are other ways to tip spiral bones but this is the most effective and quickest, once you've mastered the process.

5. Working with Spring Steel/White Bones

To work most efficiently you'll want to measure your corset or corset pattern to determine the quantity of each length of bone you'll require. Example: 8 pieces at 12" (30.5cm) and 6 pieces at 12½" (32cm), etc. Once you determine how many bones you need of each length, you can start marking the boning with an indelible marker at the intervals where you'll need to cut the bone lengths.

Cutting Spring Steel/White Bones

Note: You'll need to use bolt cutters. If the steel is wider then 8mm (³/₈") you may need to use tin snips. Bolt cutters work best on narrower steel. See Section 1 Chapter 1 for information on tin snips and bolt cutters.

1. Mark the cutting lines. Bones should be about ½" (13mm) shorter than the finished casing.

2. Align the cut mark on the steel between the jaws of the bolt cutter; squeeze, cutting across the whole piece.

3. Rest your thumb and forefinger on the steel, on either side of the bolt cutters.

4. Press down quickly to snap the steel.

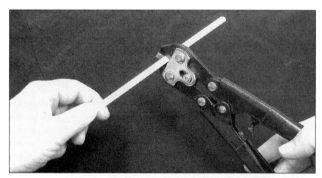

If you press slowly you'll end up with a slight bend at the tip that will create a problem for tipping and for sliding into any casing. It's very difficult to trim a small amount off this steel, so practise this technique on scrap as it does take a while to get it right.

Finishing Spring Steel/White Bones

Note: You'll need two pairs of needle-nose pliers.

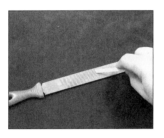 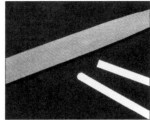

1. File the sharp corners down slightly.

2. Apply "U" tips.

   a) Place one pair of needle-nose pliers in your right hand. Place one tip, flat, between the jaws. Gently apply pressure so that you're gripping the tip but not squishing it.

   b) Pick up a bone, slide the cut end into the tip, squeeze the pliers a bit to grip the tip and the bone.

   c) Pick up the second set of pliers in your left hand, apply the jaws to either side of the tip. Apply pressure to both sets of pliers simultaneously.

If you apply pressure in only one direction the tip pops out in the opposite direction. Some people say they resort to glue to help – if you do this use

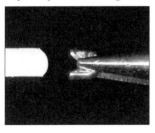 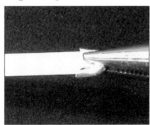

 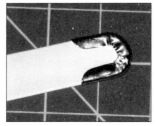

the glue sparingly. There are other ways to tip spiral bones, but this is the most effective and quickest once you've mastered the process.

Alternate method:

1. File corners down.

2. Dip the ends with "tool dip" (found at local hardware stores).

3. Let dry and reapply if needed.

The cut ends of spring steel/white steel must be finished or blunted as the ends are very sharp and may tear the fabric as you slide them into their casings. They'll definitely create holes in the garment if they aren't dulled and will cause discomfort to the wearer.

Wider steel is handled in much the same way. Measure and mark your steel as described earlier. Use tin snips to cut directly across the wide steel bone and then snip off the two corners to make the steel fit the large "U" tips better. You may need to file them as well. Now apply the "U" tips as described earlier in "Finishing Spring Steel."

To simplify the process of cutting and tipping steel bones there are machines that do both steps of the process and lessen the physical demand on your hands. These machines aren't motorized and are therefore considered a tool rather than a machine. They're easy on your hands as you're simply pulling a lever rather than squeezing a pair of handles.

Bone tipping tools aren't common but they're a great advantage if you need to cut and tip a lot of bones on a regular basis. The bone tipping tool

consists of an arbor press and specially designed dies that are engineered to fit specific dimensions of bones. The arbor press provides the force and the dies are designed to both cut and apply the "U" tips to the bones. This does require two steps – one to cut the bone and one to tip the bone, but both steps are accomplished with one die.

6. Working with an Opening Busk

An opening busk is comprised of two pieces that can separate. This allows the corset to open at the front (or wherever else you use the busk). There are straight, wide and spoon busks, and they can vary in length from about 6" to about 16".

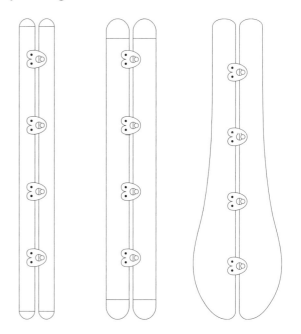

Straight, wide and spoon busks

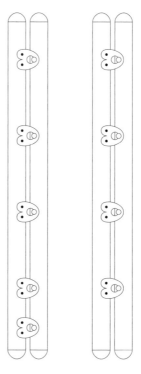

Each piece is an equal length of steel. One piece has steel busk knobs riveted onto it and the other has steel loops. The loops should line up with the knobs – always check this fact before starting to build the busk into the corset. Some busks do have a top and bottom but many can be used either way. Busks that have two knobs/loops close together at one end are busks with both a top and bottom end. The bottom end will have the two knobs/loops closer to the bottom.

Note: The knobs of the busk face outwards away from the body.

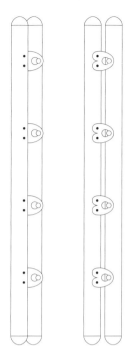

Left: Busk closed incorrectly without the space. Right: Busk closed correctly.

You'll need to notice that there *may* be two ways to fit the busk pieces together. This isn't possible with the spoon busk. Look carefully at the busk side that has the knobs. You'll notice that these knobs aren't set dead center of the busk piece but are off to one side. This is an important detail. You may find that you can turn the loop side upside down or reversed and still close the busk as the loops and knobs may still line up. However by doing this you won't have a space between the two busk pieces and this space is absolutely necessary. It's required so that there is room for the fabric that will cover the busk to fit between the two busk pieces when the busk is closed. By sewing in the busk so that there is no space you end up with a very tight fit and it may be difficult or impossible to close the busk once the corset is made up.

Spoon busks have a top and bottom end and people often mistake which end is up. The spoon busk is shaped somewhat like a spoon, with a *handle* and a *bowl*. The handle goes between the breasts and the bowl cups the stomach. A spoon busk is specific to a very short time period in the late 1800s and was considered a healthier busk because it cupped the stomach rather than flattening it. Spoon busks solve a problem common when corseting women with full abdomens, as the cupping of the busk keeps the corset neatly shaped to the body. A flat busk can create a profile similar to a ski jump as the flat busk follows the curve of the stomach outward. A spoon busk isn't the only way to solve this problem; alterations to the corset pattern can also help.

Is there a right and a left side to a busk?
I'm not sure on this, but as I'm right handed, I put the loop side of the busk on the right side of the corset, as it's easier for me to pull the right side with loops and hook them over the knobs on the left side. This means I simply need to hold the left side of the corset in place with my left hand and pull the right side over so that the loops hook over the knobs of the left side.

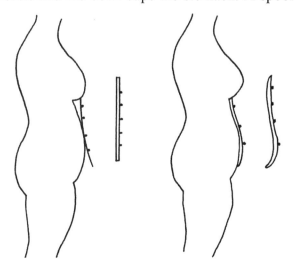

Comparison of using straight and spoon busks

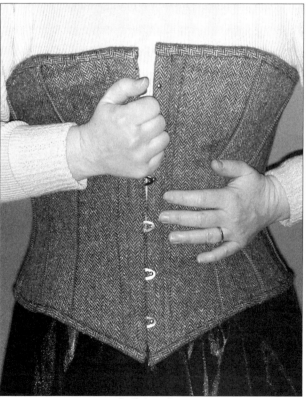

Self-dressing

The knobs and loops of busks are silver colored but can be coated with metal paint or even nail polish, though the nail polish won't be long lasting. You'll need to buff the silver areas you wish to paint with very fine sandpaper; the black type sometimes called *water paper* works well. Then either spray paint them with paint specifically for metal or use the little bottles of touch-up paint for cars. Both can be found at most hardware stores. This enables you to make the busk closure either blend with the outer fabric or contrast with it. The selection of metal paint available today is fairly extensive and you may be surprised and inspired by what you find.

How do I decide what size busk I need?
This is a common and important question. The busk size is determined by two things: the corset pattern and the body that will be wearing the corset. Some corset styles are longer than others and require longer busks; some bodies are shorter than others and require shorter busks for the same corset style.

To determine the busk length for your project you should make a mock-up of the corset pattern. A mock-up is a test garment made of cheap fabric or scraps that is used to test the fit of your pattern. You need to make a mock-up in order to discover not only the length of the busk but the length of the bones you'll need as well. Stitch your mock-up and try it on, pin it closed, and then sit down on a hard chair like a kitchen chair.

You'll need a ruler – the classic wooden ruler works well but any solid ruler will do. Place the ruler along the center front of your corset with the number 1" down near the bottom and the higher numbers up toward your chest. The ruler should start at the bottom of the corset (where the finished edge will be), and the inch measurement you can read on the ruler at the top finished edge will indicate the busk length. Busks are most commonly found in 1" increments so if your measurement is 12½" and a 12½" busk isn't available then you need a 12" busk. It's always better to go shorter and add a hook and eye than go longer and create an uncomfortable garment. Be sure you're sitting up straight when you measure your busk.

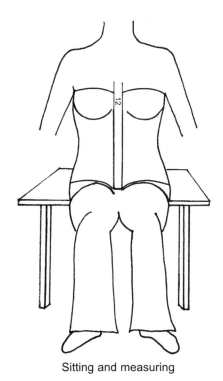

Sitting and measuring

Note: Don't measure for a busk while standing up. When we sit our body shrinks slightly and if we measure for the busk length while standing then it may not be possible to sit down without discomfort as the bottom end of the busk will press into the pubic bone. The busk should always come to the top edge of the corset.

Applying an Opening Busk

Regardless of whether you're making a single or double layer corset or which style of opening busk you're using, the application of the busk is basically the same.

Start with the loop half of the busk.

1. Pick up one front set of pieces (shell and lining or shell and facing). Place the lining/facing and shell right sides together, matching any notches.

2. Lay your busk with the loops in place along the center front seam line. Softly trace the outline of the busk and mark where the loops need to protrude through the center seam line. (A)

3. Stitch the center front seam line, leaving open spots at each loop marking. Backstitch before and after each opening. (B) *It's important that this seam is well stitched.* Press the seam open,

fold the layers back so that the wrong sides are face to face, and press the seam closed.

4. **Edge stitch** $1/16$" (1.5mm) from the edge, but avoid stitching through the gaps where the loops will have to come through. Place pins at each opening edge so you can clearly see where not to sew. (C) Slide the busk loops through the gaps and push the busk firmly into place.

5. Using a zipper foot, stitch around the busk. You may wish to pin the fabrics together. (D)

Note: The loop side has to be done first as it determines the placement of the knob side.

Once you have your loop side sewn into place, take the opposite set of fronts (shell and lining/facing) and with right sides together:

6. Stitch the center front closed. (E) Trim the shell seam allowance to $1/8$" (3mm).

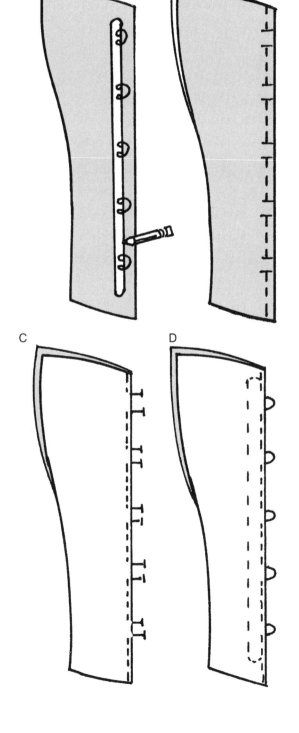

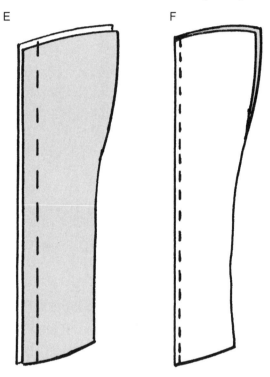

7. Press the seam open and then fold the pieces back so that wrong sides are together and press the center front edge flat. Topstitch along the edge (1/16" or 1.5mm). (F)

8. Align the previously sewn front so that the bottom and top edges line up with center fronts facing each other as they would once the corset is on the body. Use the loops as a template for marking the placement of the knobs. Mark with disappearing ink or a color pencil close to your fabric color. (G)

9. Use an awl to create holes where you've marked the placement of the knobs. (H)

10. Work the knobs through the holes created by the awl and use your fingernail to smooth out threads, if needed, at the base of each knob.

Note: The busk goes in with the knobs set closest to the busk edge along the side closest to center front.

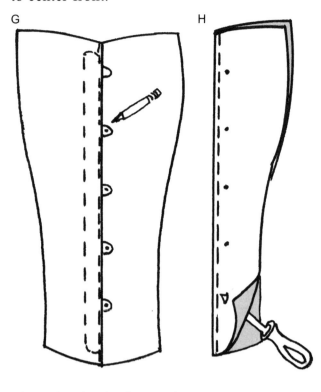

11. Slide the busk snugly into place with the front edge between the seam allowances, pin into place, and using the zipper foot stitch around the busk as done for the loop side. (I)

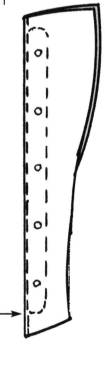

The stitch lines shown on these illustrations go around the busk to clearly indicate the shape. You could sew straight lines from the top to the bottom edge of your corset and still have a securely installed busk.

7. Setting Grommets or Eyelets (Including into Lacing Bones)

Setting grommets and eyelets by hand is the most common method of setting. If you have a machine then you should follow the instructions that came with it, and keep in mind that not all machines work the same – some require the grommet on the bottom and others require the washer on the bottom. Always check how your machine works before using it. Instructions below are for grommets and eyelets that are set with washers. The washers go on the back/facing of the fabric while the grommets and eyelets go on the right side.

Just as in applying the busk you need to first measure and mark the placement of the grommets. This is a fairly simple process. Be sure to use a see-through plastic ruler and disappearing ink or a color that blends with the fabric.

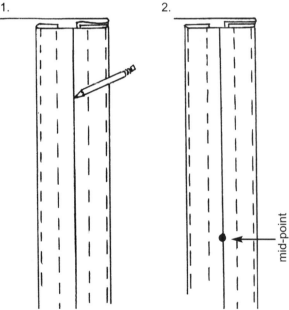

1 Draw a line parallel to the center back and in the middle of the grommet setting area, on the inside of the corset (on the facing or lining) so that no lines will be visible on the outside if your disappearing ink doesn't disappear. All your grommet placement marks should be on this line to keep them in a straight line down the center backs. If they aren't in a straight line it'll be very obvious when you're done.

2. Measure the length of the line you've just

drawn and find the mid-point. Mark it for a grommet with a dot centered on the line.

3. Mark the top and bottom grommet placement, taking into consideration your seam allowance at top and bottom. The outer edge of your grommet can't come into the seam allowance. If the seam allowance is ½" (12mm) then the grommet placement marking will be at about 1" (25mm) from the raw edge. The marking indicates the center of the grommet and you may place the marking closer or further than 1" depending on the size of the grommet and its diameter when set. Larger grommets need more space; you can lay the washers on the line to get a feel for the placement.

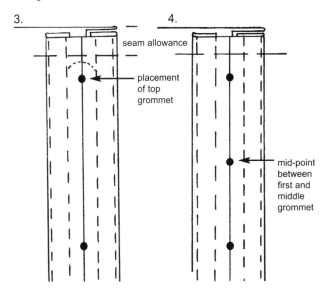

4. Once you have the middle grommet marked, and then the top and bottom grommets marked, then you use the ruler to find the middle point between the top and middle grommet, and the middle point between the bottom and middle grommet. These will be points to mark for the next grommets.

5. Repeat this process until you have all grommet placements marked and grommets are no more than about 1" (25mm) apart.

6. Punch the holes at all grommet placement markings. You may use either a hammer-style hole punch or a pliers-style hole punch. Most hammer-style grommet kits come with the hammer-style hole punch, hammer-style

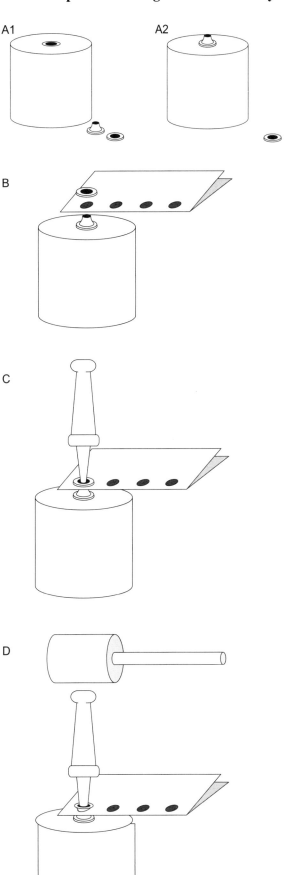

grommet setting tool, and a solid metal base. The grommet gets placed in the base with the shank facing upward. (A1, A2) The base should be on a solid surface that won't bounce or flex during the setting process. A concrete floor is good – a kitchen table isn't.

7. The fabric with the hole fits over the grommet, with the shank being forced up through the hole in the fabric. The right side of the fabric is facing the base and the wrong side or facing/lining is facing upward. (B)

8. The washer gets placed over the grommet with the convex curve facing upwards.

9. The grommet setting tool needs to have its nose placed inside the hole of the grommet shank, and once in place you hammer it with a rubber, wooden or rawhide mallet. (C, D)

Note: Don't use a steel hammer as steel on steel can be dangerous. If your grommet is set slightly lopsided you can re-insert the grommet setting tool and hammer it again, adjusting the point of pressure to create a more even set.

Remember that the more grommets you set, the less stress there is on each grommet, but more grommets require a longer lacing cord.

Setting Grommets Using Lacing Bones

To set grommets in lacing bones follow the directions for using lacing bones found in Chapter 8. When your lacing bones are in place and you're ready to set grommets or eyelets you simply follow the steps listed above. The only difference is that your grommet shank will extend through the shell fabric, the bone, and the lining fabric so you need to check the shank will be long enough to still be able to turn back on itself during the setting process. You may want to buy an extra set of lacing bones so that you can test the process. Cut scraps of the fabric you're using and just test the setting on one hole. Keep the test lacing bone so that you can test other fabrics and grommets in the holes that are left. There are some eyelets available with longer shanks but they're hard to find.

8. Applying Lacing Tape and Lacing Bones

Lacing tape is a strip of fabric that has eyelets set into it at regular intervals. The eyelets have been set by machine and don't have washers behind them. There are two types of lacing tapes: those with eyelets set along one edge, and those with eyelets set down the middle between two channels for bones on either side of the eyelets.

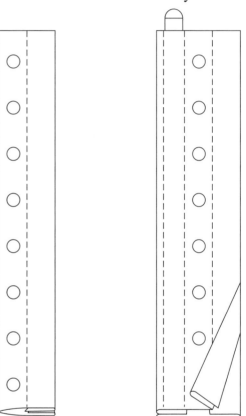

Why use lacing tape?

Lacing tape greatly reduces the time involved in setting grommets or eyelets by hand. Using lacing tape also removes the risk of poorly set and badly aligned grommets. The eyelets in lacing tape are all securely set in a straight line. So using lacing tape is a great option for those who aren't skilled at setting grommets and for those wishing to save time. Or use it **basted** into a mock-up for fitting purposes!

Lacing tape with eyelets set along one edge isn't as strong as the one with channels for bones, and while this is a perfectly adequate lacing tape for limited wear corsets, it isn't a good choice for the rigorous wear of theatre or for tight lacers. Lacing tape with bone channels is made of coutil and has a channel down either side of the eyelets for adding bones. Boning helps support the eyelets when they're under pressure from lacing. This is a better choice for theatre if you don't plan on setting your own grommets.

Applying Lacing Tape

Regardless of how you choose to sew the lacing tape on, you first need to consider making some alterations to your pattern as the eyelets of the eyelet tape should be positioned in place of where the grommets were to be. Simply sewing the lacing tape onto the center back seam won't accomplish this and will affect the fit of the corset.

1. Take your pattern back panel and lay the lacing tape upon it so that the eyelets are lined up over the grommet placement markings. This will give you the length of the lacing tape you require and will indicate how much of your back panel you need to remove. Don't cut it off – just fold it out of the way.

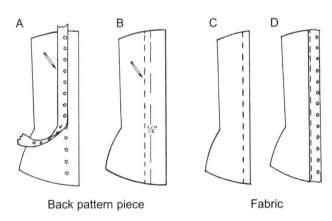

Back pattern piece   Fabric

2. With the lacing tape laying on your pattern draw a line on the pattern piece to mark the new seam where the lacing tape will be sewn to. This line will be between the grommet placement marks and the side seam. (A)

3. Remove the lacing tape from the pattern and using the line you've drawn, add the seam allowance toward the center back. Add ½" (13mm) seam allowance as this is easier to sew and then you can trim the seam allowance down to ¼" (6mm) if needed. Don't cut your pattern – just fold the pattern

along this new cutting line and use it this way to lay on your fabric and cut the fabric to this new size. Mark the stitching line at the top and bottom or write the seam allowance size within the seam allowance so you don't forget what it is. (B)

Note: Your back panel will now be smaller (C) and may look a little odd. Don't worry as you will now sew on the bone lacing tape as outlined in the next few pages. By adding the lacing tape your back panels will return to their original dimensions. (D)

Lacing Tape – Basic

Lacing tape with eyelets set down one side of the tape can be set in either of two ways:

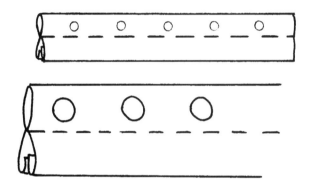

Method #1 – Sandwiched (my preferred method)

1. Lay the lacing tape on the right side of the fabric (outer layer) along the center back edge of your corset. The edge without eyelets is the seam allowance edge and this should be within the seam allowance edge along the center back. This means the eyelet edge of the lacing tape is furthest from the center back edge. Be sure that the right side of the eyelet tape is against the right side of the fabric. Yes, there is a right side of the eyelet tape so look carefully. Pin the tape in place.

2. Stitch the lacing tape into place. Use a zipper foot to allow you to get close enough to the eyelets. There is a stitching line on this lacing tape and you can use it as a guide for your stitching. (A)

3. Take your lining or facing piece and lay it on top of the piece you've just sewn, matching

any notches. Pin it into place and stitch it along the same stitching line, still using a zipper foot. You now have the lacing tape sandwiched between two layers of coutil and secured with two rows of stitching, one on top of the other. (B)

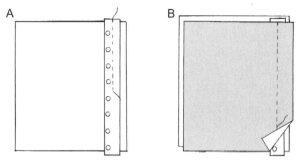

4. Fold the fabrics back away from the eyelets to expose them, press the folded fabric into place along the center back edge. Press to flatten the fold.

5. Topstitch through all layers at about $^1/16$" (1.5cm) and $^3/8$" (10mm) from the folded edge. The distance between the two rows of stitching depends on the size of bone being used. This creates a bone channel. The bone placed here will add some support to the eyelets. You now have four rows of stitching securing the lacing tape. (C)

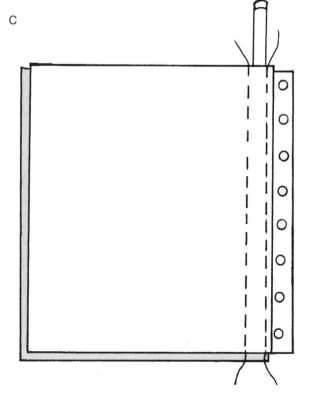

Method #2

1. Take the center back panel and the center back lining/facing and with wrong sides together stitch down the center back. (A)

2. Trim the seam allowance down to ¼" (6mm).

3. Open the only side of the eyelet tape that can be opened. (B)

4. Slide the lacing tape seam allowance over the trimmed seam allowance and stitch along the edge of the lacing tape, securing both lacing tape edges and the fabric in-between them. (B)

This method results in a neat finish (C) but is less secure than method #1 as there is only one row of stitching rather than three. You may still be able to slide a narrow bone into the seam allowance. This method is best considered for decorative purposes.

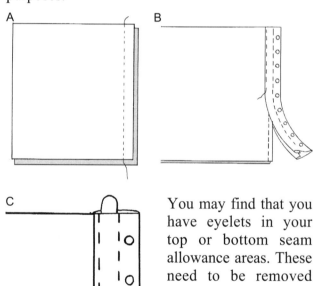

You may find that you have eyelets in your top or bottom seam allowance areas. These need to be removed before finishing your corset and can be pulled out with a pair of needle-nose pliers. Stick one jaw of the pliers through the hole of the eyelet, grasp the eyelet firmly, and pull out at an angle. It may take a bit of twisting too, but it will come out.

Lacing Tape with Bone Casings

Lacing tape with bone casings incorporated in the tape is the best lacing tape to use for corsets which will face any kind of stress; either long-term wear or tight lacing. There is only one method of applying this type of lacing tape.

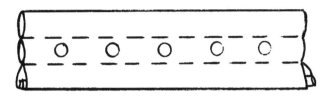

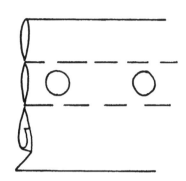

You need to adjust your pattern in a similar way as described earlier to avoid increasing the size of the corset.

This lacing tape has an edge that opens just as the previous lacing tape did, and when you open this edge you'll find that the two pieces of fabric that create it have been folded back on themselves (illustrated above.)

1. Open the folded edge of the lacing tape and place it right side to right side with the shell fabric, raw edges together and the lacing tape on top. (A)

2. Stitch in the fold line of the lacing tape. (A)

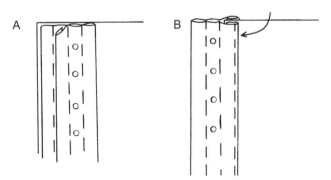

3. Flip the lacing tape over so that the raw edges which you've just sewn together are encased between the two folded edges of the lacing tape. (B)

4. Topstitch along the edge of the fold securing all layers of corset and tape. (B)

5. Slide bones into each casing. (C)

The eyelets are evenly spaced and you may find that one or two are within your top or bottom

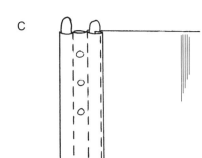

seam allowance. They must be removed prior to finishing the corset and will require the use of needle-nose pliers. Place one jaw of the pliers into the eyelet hole, grip the eyelet, and pull out at an angle. You may have to twist the eyelet and it will take a bit of effort but it can be done. The binding of the top and bottom edge will likely cover the hole that is left in the fabric where you removed the eyelets.

Applying Lacing Bones

A lacing bone is a flat strip of steel with rounded ends and several evenly spaced holes down the entire length of the strip. It's used in the back of a corset to add support to the grommets/eyelets. By using a lacing bone your grommets or eyelets are set in steel that's covered with corset fabric. It's virtually impossible for the grommets to get pulled out of the corset during lacing or extended wear as they're anchored in the steel rather than just in fabric. Using lacing bones removes the need for two bones down either side of the grommets as usually required in corset building.

1. Sew the center back seam as usual. (You need two layers of fabric for the lacing bone to slide between; more than two layers may be a problem depending on the length of the shank of your grommets.) Press the seam flat, then press it open and flip it so that wrong sides are together. Press the folded edge, and edge stitch at $1/16$" (1.5mm).

2. With your fabric right side up, lay the lacing bone on the fabric in the position it should be on the finished garment. Use the lacing bone as a template to mark your grommet placements on both right and left back pieces. (A)

3. Remove the lacing bone. Punch the holes according to your kit or machine. Note that you're going through all layers of fabric. (B)

Note: Removing a grommet or eyelet from a lacing bone is next to impossible so work carefully.

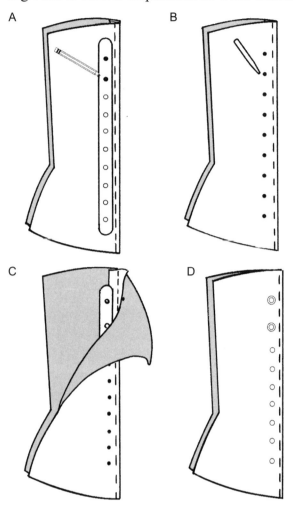

4. Slide the lacing bone into place so that the holes in the fabric align with the holes in the bones. You'll have fabric on both sides of the bone. (C)

5. Place a grommet or eyelet through a hole going neatly through the outer layer or fabric shell, bone, and lining or facing. Check that the shank of the grommet or eyelet is coming all the way through and will be long enough to get its rim rolled during the setting process. You may find that you can't use a washer with lacing bones but as they're set in steel the washer isn't so important. This will depend on the layers and thickness of your fabric and the length of your eyelets.

6. Set the grommet or eyelet as usual. Then set the rest of them. (D)

9. Applying Lace Tips

Lace tips are the things that are attached to the end of corset laces or cords of any kind, to stop them from fraying and keep them tight so the laces can be passed through eyelet and grommet holes.

Lace tips come in two forms: metal (which are usually referred to as aglets and require a special tool to apply), and plastic or shrink tips which shrink onto lace/cord with the application of heat. The tool required to apply aglets tends to be fairly expensive and will likely come with instructions. The shrink tips are very economical and easy to use but hard to find and don't always come with instructions.

Applying Shrink Tips

1. You'll need a needle and thread, the color of which should match your corset lace or cord.

2. Using the needle and thread bind the end of the cord and *don't* cut the thread.

3. Cut a piece of the tubing about ½"(13mm).

4. Trim the fluff end so it fits through the shrink tube, but don't cut the thread.

5. Drop the needle that you used to bind the cord end, and that is still attached to the cord, down through the tube.

6. Slowly pull on the needle, pulling the bound cord into the tube until the shrink tube covers the end of the cord. Still don't cut the thread.

7. Hold the tube close to a candle or a hot iron and watch the tube begin to shrink. Watch as the texture of the cord becomes visible on the tube as this indicates the tube is shrinking to the point of contact. It's easiest to hold the tube close to a heat source if you haven't yet cut the thread and needle off. Hold the needle in one hand and the cord in the other to keep the tube level with the heat source.

8. Once you've shrunk the tip and it has cooled, give it a tug and be sure it's secure. *Now* cut the thread and needle off and trim the end of the tube if needed. Repeat the process with the other end of the lacing cord.

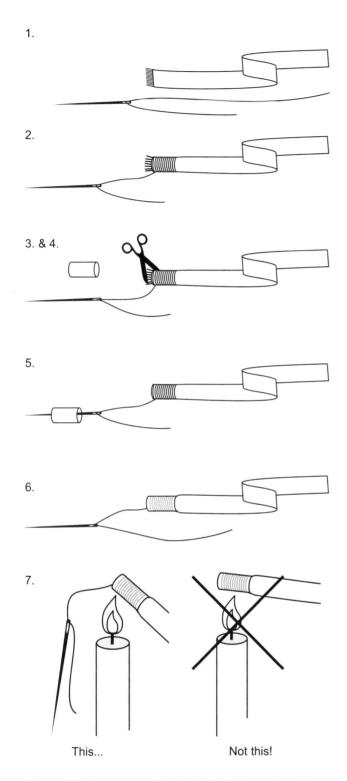

1.

2.

3. & 4.

5.

6.

7.

This...   Not this!

Note: If using a candle don't hold the tube above the flame as it'll get sooty and gray – hold it beside the candle. I prefer to use an iron as it's usually already on and I don't like the idea of a burning candle in my sewing room! Heat guns can be used but some are too hot and the tip almost liquefies and is ruined.

10. Lacing a Corset

It may be surprising to discover that there are a few ways to lace a corset, and that how it's done may affect the placement of your grommets. Most corsets throughout time have been laced up the center back and that's what will be described here. You can apply these principles to lacing anywhere on any garment.

Before choosing a lacing technique you may ask, "Do I start lacing from the top or from the bottom?" The answer is – "That depends." I've heard a theory that the Elizabethans laced from the top down to attain a flatter chest. And other periods increased the height of the chest by lacing from the bottom up. I lace all of my corsets from the top down as this allows me to tuck the ends of the cord out of sight (up inside the bottom edge of my corset) and it's easier if I have to dress myself.

Single Cord Lacing

This uses a **single cord** with one end anchored to the corset and the other end threading through the grommets/eyelets. This form of lacing seems to

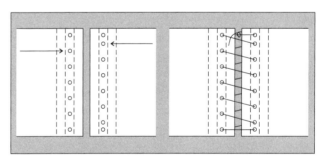

Grommet placement   Threading

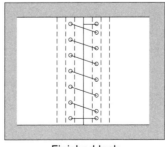

Finished look

be referred to in earlier corsets up to the Regency period. I've read and heard that some people consider it an easier lacing technique for anyone who is dressing themselves, but my experience is contrary to this. I've made only one corset with this form of lacing as I found it to be exceptionally awkward – even when lacing it up on a dress form.

Section Two: Building a Corset

Note: The grommets aren't placed directly opposite each other along the center back pieces, but are offset halfway between one another.

Double Cord Lacing

This term is a bit misleading as it *is* done with a single cord; but both ends get threaded through the grommets. This is the most common form of lacing and requires that the grommets/eyelets be placed opposite one another up the center back panels. The grommet placement for **double cord lacing** is always the same in that the grommets are always opposite each other along the parallel center back pieces. However how the laces are threaded through the grommets can vary.

The most common double cord lacing is the basic criss-cross method, and while this is familiar to most people you may not have noticed that there is a method to be followed – not as simple as it may look. It's especially easy to miss a grommet.

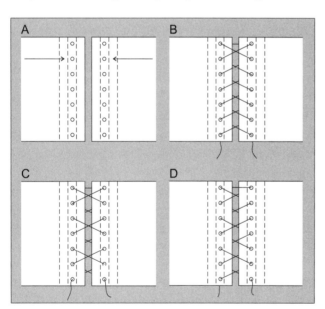

A) Grommet placement   B) Lacing from the top
C) Lacing from the top, another method
D) What it looks like if you're not consistent.

This is the most basic lacing technique but not necessarily the best or most functional. Using this technique but making one little change makes it easier to dress yourself alone and gives better waist definition. Add rabbit ears at the waist. By lacing the corset so that there are two long loops (the rabbit ears) you make it easy to tighten the corset yourself. It can be loosely laced

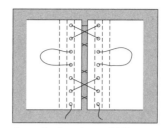

Laced, showing rabbit ears

so that it's easy to get into; the bottom of the lace can be tied. Once the busk is closed at center front you can reach around, grab the two loops and gently pull them until the corset is comfortably tight. Pulling the corset ties this way tightens both above and below the waist evenly and easily. It also allows you to control the comfort level by yourself.

Without changing the grommet placement you can create more decorative lacing looks, less functional as they may be and more difficult to tighten, but if you're considering your corset for outerwear you may not be concerned with function.

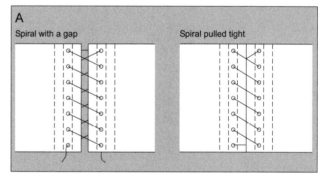

A
Spiral with a gap   Spiral pulled tight

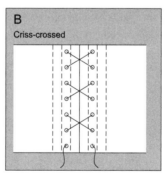

B
Criss-crossed

Lacing affects the center back seams. As lacing is pulled tight it creates stress on the grommets or eyelets and this can misshape the back seams. The use of strong bones down the center back helps to avoid this problem.

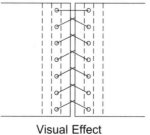

Visual Effect
with bones

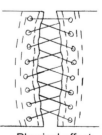

Physical effect
No or weak bones

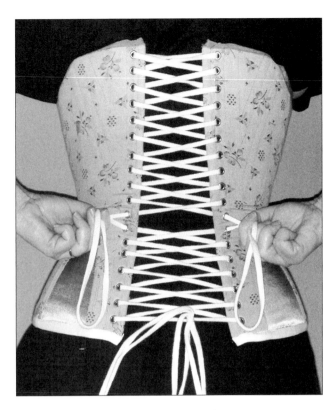

Self dressing, pulling rabbit ears

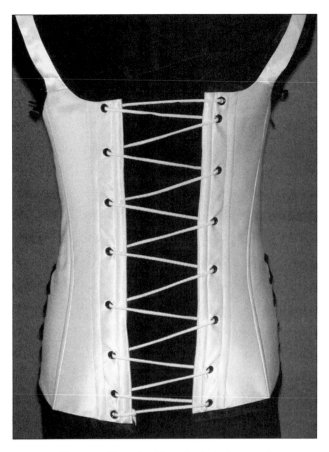

Regency Corset with a single lacing cord

Corset laced from the top

11. Making and Applying Bias Tape and Petersham Ribbon

Bias tape can be any width and it's a simple strip of fabric that has been cut on the bias of the fabric rather than with or across the grain. Some bias tapes come prefolded but you'll likely make your own so that it matches your corset fabric. Contrasting bias tape can be an attractive and simple design feature and can be made of any fabric.

Bias tape is commonly used to bind the top and bottom edges of a corset to finish these edges. The important characteristic of bias tape is its ability to stretch and shrink to accommodate both concave and convex curves without puckering or pulling. An ordinary ribbon doesn't respond the same way and can't be used to bind the curved edges.

A cotton or cotton/viscose petersham ribbon will work but you need to be sure it's a real petersham ribbon and not polyester. Many terms are misused and you may think what you're buying is petersham ribbon and it's not. The right petersham ribbon won't have smooth selvedges. The edges will be bumpy. If they're smooth then there is a woven selvedge to stabilize the ribbon and it won't stretch and shrink as needed. Bias tape will always work and is the best product for the novice corset maker to use.

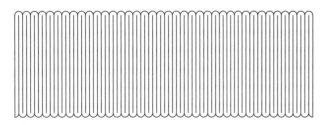

Petersham ribbon

Test your choice in ribbon before sewing. It should pin neatly into place without puckering or pulling. The visual effect of your bias binding will change with the width of the bias binding you use and the size of the seam allowance. You'll get a wider flatter look if you use a wider bias binding. Sew a ½" (13mm) seam allowance and don't trim it down, and you'll get a smaller more three-dimensional look if you use narrower binding, or trim the seam allowance down and use the double bias method.

Making Your Own Bias Tape

This is simple if you have the right tools: a 2" wide see-through ruler and rotary cutter or scissors.

First: Do the Math!

For Single Bias Binding

Bias tape needs to be at least *four times* the desired finished width of the binding. Add ¼" (6mm) to ³⁄₈" (9mm) total to help with the stretching and easing you may have to accommodate when binding curves.

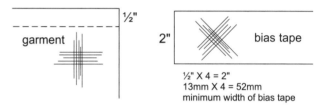

½" X 4 = 2"
13mm X 4 = 52mm
minimum width of bias tape

For Double Bias Binding

Bias tape needs to be at least *six times* the desired finished width of the binding. Add ¼" (6mm) to ³⁄₈" (9mm) total to help with the stretching and easing you may have to accommodate when binding curves.

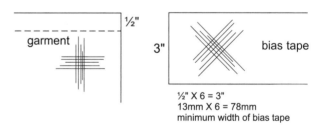

½" X 6 = 3"
13mm X 6 = 78mm
minimum width of bias tape

1. Decide on the width of bias tape you want. This depends on your seam allowance at top and bottom, what kind of effect you want, and which method of binding you choose, either single or double. Assuming the seam allowance is ½" (13mm) and you're using the single bias method, then you'll need bias tape that is at least 2" (50mm) wide plus ¼" (6mm) for a total width of 2¼" or 56mm.

2. Spread your fabric out on the table. It should be pressed and wrinkle free. Your see-

through ruler should have small squares on it and you can line these squares up with the selvedge so it's running diagonally through the squares.

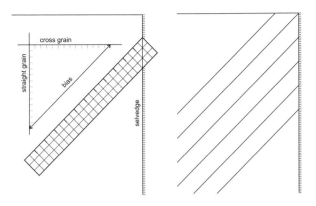

Marking bias strips on your fabric

3. Use disappearing ink or chalk to draw the lines on both sides of the ruler for the first strip and use one of these lines to line up your ruler for the next strip. Repeat to get the number of strips you require.

Note: You may want to measure the lengths of the top and bottom edges to see what lengths you'll need. If the lengths are longer than what you can get in one piece of bias tape, then you'll need to piece the bias tape before sewing it onto your corset.

4. Cut the bias strips along the lines you've drawn.

5. If you need to piece them together do so by using the angles already found at either end. Don't cut these angles off as you need to sew the pieces together on the straight grain to keep the stretch characteristic.

Join ends on the straight grain to piece strips

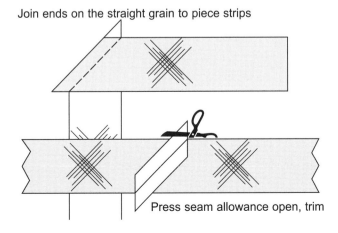

Press seam allowance open, trim

Applying Bias Tape

There are two basic methods of applying bias tape to a garment; single and double binding. Double binding is sometimes known as *French binding*.

Single Binding

1. With right sides together and raw edges aligned stitch the bias tape to the edge of the corset, having folded back the end of the tape so that it will be encased within the bias binding when finished. You're stitching along the seam line.

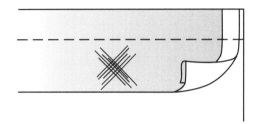

2. Flip the bias tape over the seam allowance.

3. Press the bias tape seam.

4. Fold the raw edge of the bias tape toward the raw edge of the corset.

5. Roll the folded bias tape over the seam

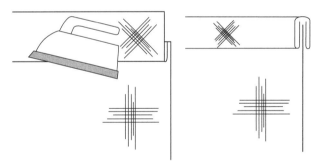

allowance so that the folded edge is on your stitching line that attached the bias tape to the corset.

6. Hand stitch the folded edge into place, on the wrong side.

Double Binding

1. Fold the bias tape down the center lengthwise, wrong sides together, raw edges together.

41.

2. Place the bias tape on the edge of the corset (right sides together) with the raw edges of the bias tape lined up with the raw edge of the corset. Fold back the front and back ends so they'll be encased in the bias tape once it's sewn into place. Stitch the bias tape to the corset along the seam line, stitching through both layers of bias tape and the corset.

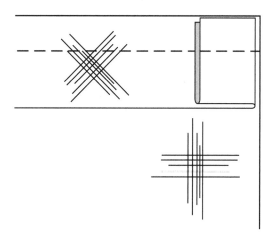

3. Flip the bias tape toward the raw edges and roll it over the edge to the inside of the corset. The folded edge should come to the stitching line you've just sewn.

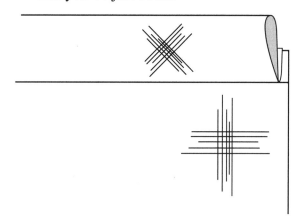

4. Hand stitch the folded edge of the bias tape in place on the wrong side.

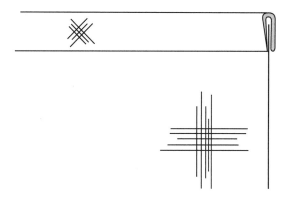

Both methods have been illustrated using 2" wide bias tape, a common size available for purchase at most retail stores. Notice the different effects.

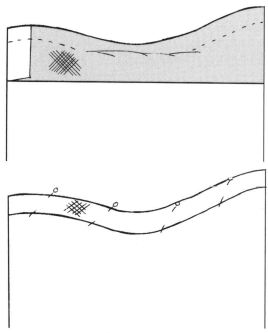

Applying single bias binding to a curve

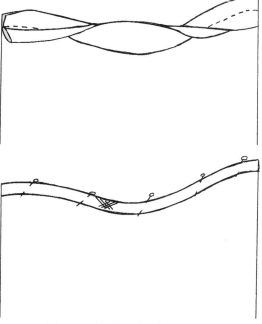

Applying double bias binding to a curve

Applying Petersham Ribbon

Petersham ribbon can also be used to bind your corset edges and is even simpler to use than bias tape. Petersham ribbon can be difficult to find and good color matches may be impossible so bias is often a better choice as it can be made out of the same fabric as your corset.

If you do choose to use petersham ribbon the 1" (25mm) wide size is a good choice.

1. Cut a length of petersham ribbon the length of the edge you need to bind plus 1" (25mm). The 1" is to allow both ends to be tucked back by ½" (13mm) each.

2. Press the petersham ribbon in half lengthwise.

3. Fold one end of the ribbon under by ½" (13mm).

4. Start pinning the ribbon in place.

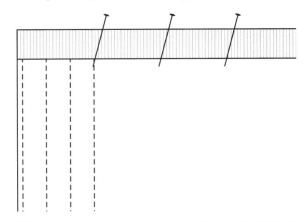

5. When you get to the opposite end fold it under. The ends should line up with the front and back edges of the corset.

6. Machine stitch the ribbon, with right side of corset up, catching both edges of ribbon on the right side and the wrong side. Be very careful not to hit a bone! You can hand stitch

this if you're unsure about catching the edges of the ribbon on both right and wrong sides.

7. Hand stich the ends closed. Leave the front top end open for your **drawcord**.

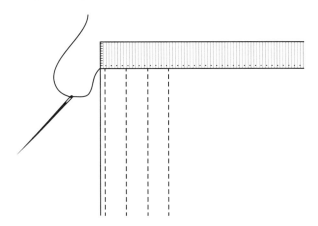

The front, back, top and bottom edges should line up evenly.

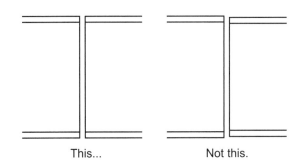

This...   Not this.

Check this before you sew the binding onto your second side. It will be very obvious if the top or bottom edges don't line up at the center front and center back.

Section Three: Construction Techniques

There are three basic methods of corset construction and two variations for each construction method will be discussed in the following chapters:

- Single layer corset (alterable and non-alterable)
- Double layer corset (alterable and non-alterable)
- Fashion fabric corset (with and without visible bone casings).

Before constructing anything it's a good idea to know what the end result should look like and what the components are. Previous chapters have discussed many of the components in detail – now you have to put them all together. You may want to refer to the Corset Map on page 2.

1. Making a Modesty Panel

A **modesty panel** or placket isn't found on many period corsets but can be added behind the laces of contemporary corsets. This is a definite addition to a bridal or evening corset that is worn as outerwear. A modesty panel is simply a rectangular piece of fabric that matches the shell of your corset and gets sewn to the inside of the back to do two things: protect the skin from the laces and hide the skin from view.

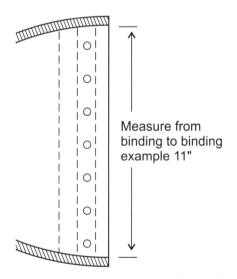

A. Length from binding to binding= 11"
11" + ½" + ½" = 12" high
(½" top & bottom seam allowances)

1. Begin by measuring the length of the back of your finished corset. Measure from the sewn edge of the top binding to the sewn edge of the bottom binding. (Example shows 11".) To cut a panel to fit this length you need to add ½" for seam allowance at each end. The total length of the panel you'll cut will therefore be 12". (A)

2. Measure the distance from the center back edge to the inside edge of the second bone. The modesty panel fits behind the grommets or eyelets so you're measuring from the back edge past the first bone, past the grommets, and just past the second bone. (B)

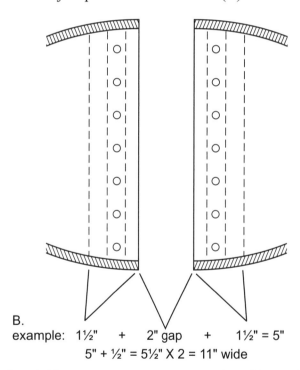

B.
example: 1½" + 2" gap + 1½" = 5"
5" + ½" = 5½" X 2 = 11" wide

3. Add your measurements together. Example: 2" for the standard gap width, 1½" for the center back edge to the second bone on the right side, and 1½" from the center back edge to the second bone on the left side, and a small seam allowance of no more than ½". Your number sentence will look like this: 2+1½ + 1½ + ½ = 5½". Now multiply the answer by 2 as you need to be able to fold it in half – and the width is 11". (B)

4. Based on these measurements you'll cut a panel that is 12" long (tall or vertical) and 11" wide. (C)

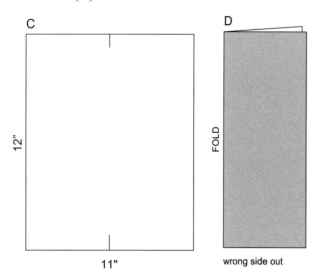

C

12"

11"

D

FOLD

wrong side out

5. Fold the panel in half from top to bottom with right sides together – check that you've folded it correctly by placing it on the back of the corset. (D)

6. Stitch along the top and bottom edge using the seam allowance you chose – in this case ½". (E)

7. Press the stitching. Turn the piece right side out and carefully poke the corners out. Press the whole piece so that it lays flat and neat. Serge the raw edges together. (F)

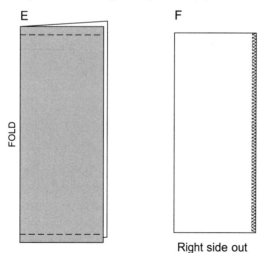

E

FOLD

F

Right side out

8. Hand stitch the serged edge of the panel to the corset along the second bone casing from center back. Don't let your stitching go through to the right side. (G)

9. The modestly panel is now in place, and will hide the flesh behind the lacing and limit any abrasion caused when the laces are pulled through the grommets to tighten the corset. (H)

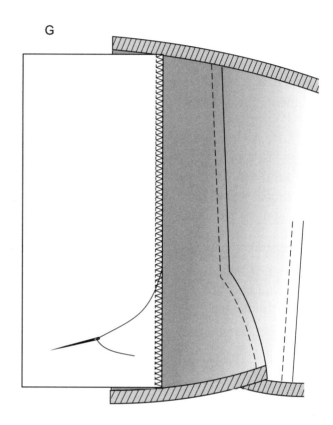

G

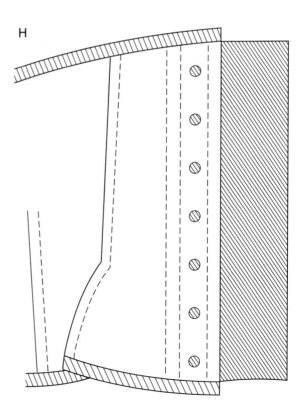

H

This photo shows the use of a modesty panel down the back of the corset. A modesty panel can be added to any corset no matter what construction technique is used.

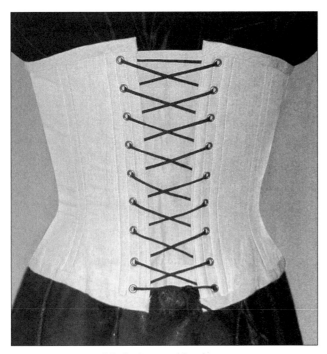

Modesty panel in place

Always, *always* follow any instructions that come with the commercial corset pattern. Whoever wrote the instructions likely had something to do with the pattern and designing how it goes together. So use their instructions over the ones described in the next few pages.

2. Making a Mock-up

A mock-up is also known as a muslin because mock-ups are often made from muslin (which is also known as factory cotton and is inexpensive unbleached cotton). A mock-up is essentially a test garment that you make from any scrap or cheap fabric you have on hand before you even cut the real thing. The point of making a mock-up is to test the fit and style of a garment on the body it's being made for. You baste a mock-up together leaving off details such as trims, buttons and grommets. You try the mock-up on and have an assistant mark any alterations with marking pen or pencil. You may let out seams by pulling out your basting thread or take them in by pinning them tighter. Whatever alterations need to be made are done when you fit the mock-up. You may fit the mock-up more than once if there are several or extreme alterations. You'll also fit the final garment before you finish it.

Why bother with a mock-up, it takes so much extra time?
A mock-up will save you frustration, money and possibly time, particularly when corset building. Corset supplies are not cheap and corsets are not quick projects, so it makes sense to get it right the first time you work with your good materials. The mock-up will help minimize problems later. For example: you discover the corset doesn't come quite high enough to cover the nipples. If you've already cut your good fabric – you can't lengthen it! This is only one possibility and there are many. *Always make a mock-up.*

How do I make a mock-up?
Before you cut the pattern pieces out you need to decide if you'll be fitting the mock-up using lacing tape at the center back, or if you just want to be able to pin the center back closed.

Note: Read the following instructions before cutting your mock-up out, particularly step #4. After you've read these instructions start by cutting out a single layer of muslin or scrap fabric. The fabric choice should be something stable such as **broadcloth**.

Section Three: Construction Techniques

1. Use the information in Section 2 Chapter 1 to label your pieces.

2. Baste all the pieces together including center front, leaving the center back open.

3. Baste lacing tape to both center backs unless you used the extension method (see step #4 below). For details on lacing tape see Section 2 Chapter 8.

4. Extension method means you add a temporary extension to both center back seams. The corset is designed to have a 2" (5cm) gap down the center back between the two center back seams. You need to close this gap for fitting unless you baste lacing tape in place or set grommets. (Why waste the grommets or time setting them?) To close the gap so you can pin the center back during fitting, you need to add a 2" (5cm) extension to both center back seams, and draw on the center line as a guide for pinning the mock-up closed.

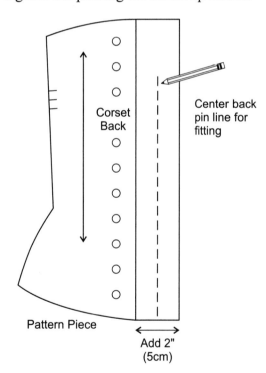

Pattern Piece

Corset Back

Center back pin line for fitting

Add 2" (5cm)

You're done making the mock-up for the first fitting! You may notice that this hasn't taken very long but will be well worth the little effort it took.

For details on fitting your mock-up skip to Section 4 Chapter 2.

3. Building a Single Layer Corset

A single layer corset is the simplest corset to make, but don't let this statement deceive you into thinking that making a single layer corset is a quick and easy project. It's easy to sew but a challenge to construct – at least the first time. So don't plan to make it today and wear it tonight. Give yourself time.

1. Cut the pieces out and be sure to cut the right quantity. The pattern may have front and back facings but may require you to cut extra front or back pieces and use them as facings. Be sure to check the pattern pieces to see if any of them say "Cut 4."

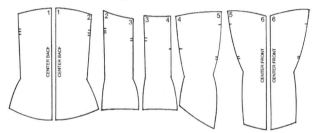

One side of corset only with full front and back facings

2. Mark the bone casings on the wrong side of the corset panels according to the pattern. Use a tracing wheel and tracing paper in a color that contrasts subtly with the fabric. The wrong side is the inside. Also trace your waistline onto the fabric at this time if the waistline is marked on the pattern pieces.

3. Label all of your pieces. Each piece should be labeled clearly within the seam allowance in numerical order so that you can easily identify the pieces in the sequence in which they need to be sewn together. See Section 2 Chapter 1.

4. Apply your busk as outlined in Section 2 Chapter 6 and complete your back panel and facing as described in the pattern instructions, or by using any of the techniques described in this book under "grommets" or "lacing tape." See Section 2 Chapters 7 and 8.

5. Sew casings on the panels using your traced-on lines as a guide, and stitching by machine along both edges of each casing. You'll have to leave this step until after the panels are sewn together if you're going to apply a waist stay. Otherwise it's easier to sew these casings on before you sew the pieces together. Remember that the stitching of the bone cas-

ings will be seen on the outside so be neat.

6. Sew your panels together following the numbers in the seam allowances. Confirm that all pieces are sewn in the correct order and then try the corset on to check the fit. If you need to make any alterations this is the time to make them.

7. You may want to stitch your seams again using a different stitch length so that your seams are double stitched. Consider stitch lengths of 8 and 12 stitches per inch.

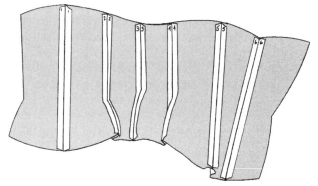

A corset panel: all pieces for one side

8. Press seams flat, together. Then press seams to one side in the direction suggested in the pattern instructions. They *won't* be pressed open. (Seams are shown open in illustration above to show clear identification of labeling.)

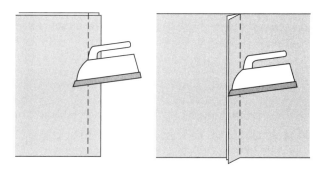

Single Layer Alterable Corset

The following instructions will give you a corset that can be altered. Serge the seam allowances together. (A) Stitch the seam allowance down to the corset by stitching along the serged edge. (B)

Your seam allowance needs to be at least ½" (13mm) wide for this and your bones need to be only ¼" (6mm) wide. You can't apply a waist stay to this type of finish as it won't allow the bones to slide through the casings.

Close-up view shows the seam allowance serged

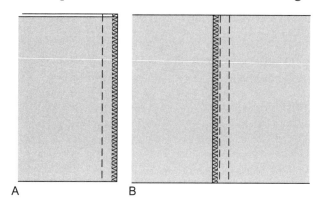

A   B

and sewn down flat against your fabric (C) and with a bone slid into the casing that was created. (D) Note the bone is between the two layers of seam allowance – which means there is one layer of fabric between the bone and the body, and two layers between the bone and the "outside" world.

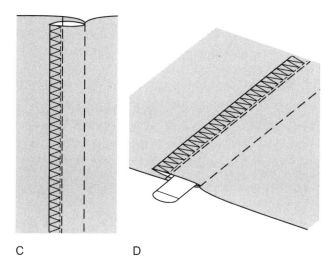

C   D

Note: When you need to alter the corset you'll need to unpick the stitching that forms the seam allowance into a bone casing, as well as unpicking the seam. Letting out the corset may mean the seam allowance isn't large enough to make a new bone casing. You may need to apply bone casing tape. When a corset needs to be let out you'll have to replace the bias binding along the top and/or bottom edge with a new longer piece.

Continue to Step #12 to complete your alterable corset.

Single Layer Non-Alterable Corset –

Beautifully Finished Inside and Out

9. Trim your seam allowances to about ½" (13mm) and ³/₈" (10mm). This means the seam allowances are graded and this decreases the bulk under the bone casing tape. (A, B)

10. If you're applying a waist stay, do so now.

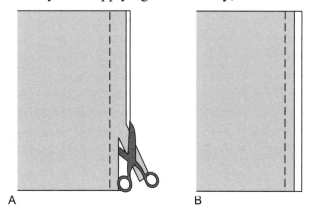

Center a length of twill tape or petersham ribbon over the drawn-on waistline. Stitch along both edges. Remember this stitching will be seen on the outside of the corset – so be neat.

11. Sew on the bone casings over the seam

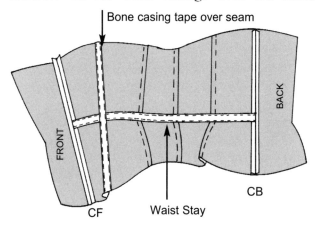

allowances. This covers any raw edges. Line up the bone casing with the seam stitching and sew by machine, first along the side closest to the seam and then along the other side. (C)

12. Stitch along the bottom edge of your corset ¼" (6mm) to ½" (13mm) depending on the width of the bias tape you're using to finish the corset.

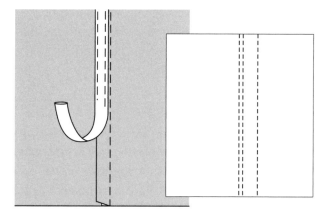

C. Applying bone casing, wrong side (insert shows right side)

13. Slide your bones into the casings to check the lengths. You'll have measured your corset for bone lengths when you finished your mock-up. For more details on bones see Section 2 Chapters 2, 3, 4 or 5.

14. Try the corset on to test the fit. If you need more support you can still add more bone casings and more bones. Remove the bones. You may want to label them so you know where they go later.

15. Finish the bottom edge of the corset with bias tape as described in Section 2 Chapter 11. You may need to trim the top and bottom edge to create a nice smooth line.

16. Slide your bones back into the correct casings.

17. Take your lengths of cable cord or ribbon and tack one end of each securely to the center back of each top edge of your corset. (A)

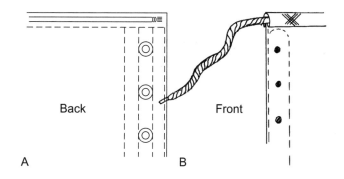

18. Finish the top edge of the corset with bias tape the same way you finished the bottom edge, encasing your cable cord or ribbon but not catching it in your stitching. The cord or ribbon needs to be able to move through the casing in order to gather it up. (B) To finish the ends of your cords see Section 2 Chapter 9.

19. If you didn't use lacing tape you'll need to set the grommets down the center back. See Section 2 Chapter 7 for instructions.

20. Lace the lacing cord through the eyelets or grommets in the back and your corset is ready to wear. See Section 2 Chapter 10 for lacing techniques.

Your Single Layer Corset is complete and ready to wear.

4. Building a Double Layer Corset

There are two methods of building a double layer corset:

- An alterable corset built to allow access to the seams so the inside has visible seam allowances. This method can't have a waist stay and seam allowances must be at least ½" (13mm). If you plan on altering the corset regularly for rental or theatrical use then you may want to consider larger than usual seam allowances.

- A corset finished as beautifully on the inside as on the outside but is virtually impossible to alter – or at least not likely worth the time and effort. The lining is very smooth against the body.

Why make a double layer corset?

A double layer corset can be more supportive and withstand harder wear as it's made with two layers of coutil. Your corset can look as beautiful on the inside as it does on the outside – important for couturier corsets. You don't need bone casing tape.

You start out the same way for either type of double layer corset.

1. You need to start by cutting four of each pattern piece – you won't need any facings. This means you have one left side outer layer (shell), one right side outer layer (shell), one left inside layer (lining), and one right inside layer (lining).

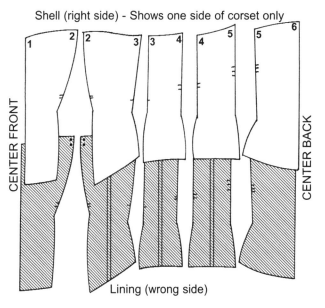

Shell (right side) - Shows one side of corset only

Lining (wrong side)

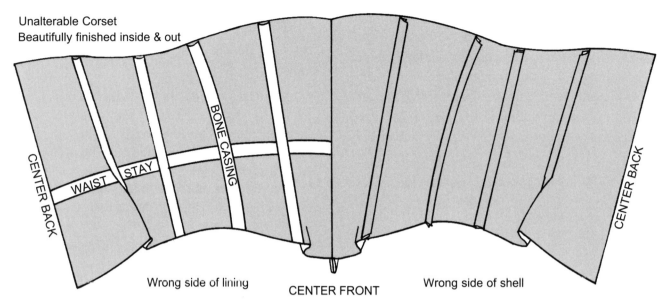

Unalterable Corset
Beautifully finished inside & out

CENTER BACK

WAIST STAY

BONE CASING

CENTER BACK

Wrong side of lining   CENTER FRONT   Wrong side of shell

2. Before removing the pattern pieces from your fabrics label each piece in the top corner within the seam allowance. Keep the labeling simple but be sure not to omit this step as it's very easy to get the pieces mixed up and even sewn on upside down! Label them in the order that they go together as this is the whole point of labeling – keeping construction simple. You can start with 1,2,3, etc., or use dots. This was discussed in detail in Section 2 Chapter 1.

3. Mark your bone casing lines on the *right side* of the lining pieces in chalk or a color that will blend with the fabric. You'll need to be able to see them once the shell and lining are attached.

Note: Once the lining is sewn to the shell you won't be able to see the bone casing lines unless you've marked them on the right side (as they will be against the shell fabric), so as much as you may want to mark them on the wrong side – don't. If you'll be applying a waist stay you can mark the waistline on the *right side* of the lining pieces, using placement from the first fitting of the mock-up or from the pattern.

4. Lay out the pieces in order on the table. Lay each pattern piece side by side in the order they'll be sewn. You'll have all of your left side pattern pieces for both shell and lining, and all of your right side pieces for both shell

and lining, and there will be your labels in each top corner on *all* pieces.

5. Assuming you've already made the mock-up you can now apply the busk as described in Section 2 Chapter 6 using all four front pieces. The front lining pieces will be treated like facings.

Double Layer Alterable Corset

Continue to step #6.

Beautiful Finish Corset

Skip to step #16.

6. Lay all of the shell pieces, wrong side up, in order of assembly on a table.

7. Take the rest of the coordinating lining pieces and lay them on top of the shell pieces wrong side down, so the wrong sides are together and each shell piece is matched with its lining piece.

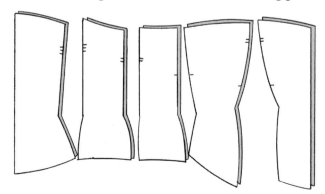

8. Pick up the back pieces and turn them so they have right sides together. Pin the shell pieces

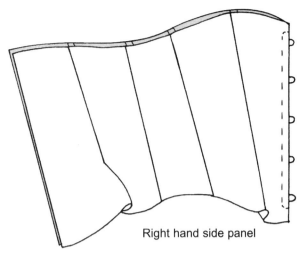

Right hand side panel

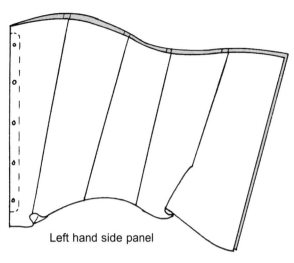

Left hand side panel

to the lining pieces with right sides still together. Stitch the center back seam. Press the seam flat, (A) then press it open. (B) Flip the lining into place so that the "wrong sides" are together. Press the folded seam. (C)

your non-on-seam bone casings now, and should be able to see the lines you drew on the right side of the lining in step #3. Simply sew along each of these lines to create a casing between the two layers of fabric. (B)

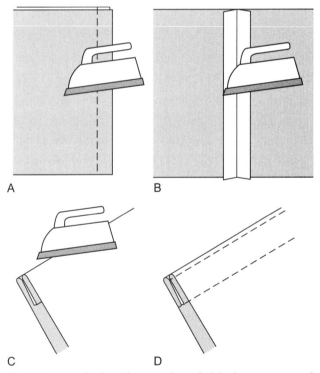

A

B

C   D

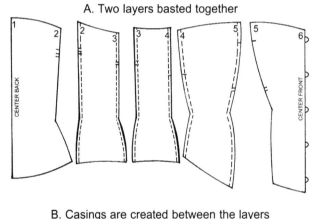

A. Two layers basted together

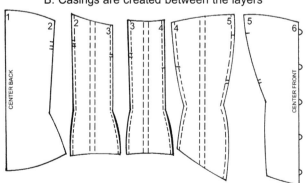

B. Casings are created between the layers

9. Edge stitch along the folded seam and machine baste the side seams together within the seam allowance. Stitch the center back bone casing as marked on your pattern. (D)

10. Pin each lining piece to the corresponding shell piece and stitch each set together by machine stitching just inside the seam allowance along each side, leaving the top and bottom edges open. (A) You can stitch

Note: You've already dealt with your front and back pieces.

11. The lining and shell pieces will now be treated as one layer. Machine stitch all pieces together in the correct order – watch your labels. Check that all pieces are in the right

order and that the two panels you have are identical in shape.

12. Sew each of your seams a second time using a different length stitch, as this will strengthen the seam and it'll be less likely to rip like a perforated stamp. Consider 8 stitches per inch and 12 stitches per inch.

13. Now serge each set of seam allowances together. (A)

14. Press all your seams in the direction as suggested in the pattern instructions. (B)

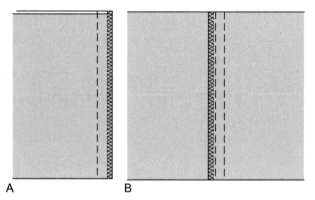

A   B

15. Chances are the seam allowance is at least ½" (13mm) and this means you can use the seam allowance as your bone casing. Stitch it down to your corset by stitching along the inside edge of the serging. (C) Your bone will slide down in-between the two layers of seam allowance – later. (D)

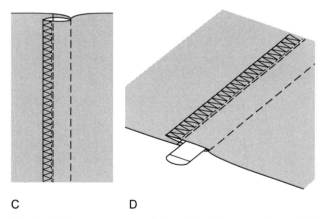

C   D

Note: When you need to alter the corset you'll need to unpick the stitching that forms the seam allowance into a bone casing, as well as unpicking the seam. Letting out the corset may mean the seam allowance isn't large enough to make a new bone casing. You may need to simply stitch a line

through the two layers of coutil parallel to the seam and use it as a casing. When a corset needs to be let out you'll have to replace the bias binding along the top and/or bottom edge with a new longer piece.

To finish your alterable corset skip to step #33.

Double Layer Corset – Beautiful Finish Inside and Out

16. Sew your pieces together in the labeled order making sure that no piece gets sewn on upside down. It sounds easy enough but I've seen many errors in sewing the pieces together, upside down, right panel number into the wrong side of the corset meaning a panel from the right side was sewn into the left side. To do this the mis-sewn piece has to be wrong side out *or* a lining piece. The pieces are almost impossible to identify and you may not discover you've made a mistake until you try to fit the corset – so watch the labels!

Note: You'll end up with only two panels each with one side of a busk in the middle.

17. Once the sewing is complete lay the corset out to assure yourself all the pieces are in the right order. The two panels should be mirror images of each other. (Illustrated at top of page 53.)

If they aren't then you have to take your pattern pieces and lay them out to discover where you went wrong and then unpick the seam. Watch your labels to avoid this problem. When you lay the panels on top of one another, as they'll eventually be sewn, check that they fit – that the lining is the same size as the shell. If there is a discrepancy fix it before you go any further.

Slight variations of seam allowance will cause the shell and lining to be different sizes. This presents a problem in the finished garment: a) if the shell is larger than the lining the shell will pucker, and b) if the lining is larger than the shell you'll get wrinkles inside which will cause discomfort to the wearer.

18. Sew each of your seams a second time using a different length stitch, as this will

strengthen the seam and it'll be less likely to rip like a perforated stamp. Consider 8 stitches per inch and 12 stitches per inch.

19. Press all your seams. All lining seams get pressed toward center front and all shell seams get pressed toward center back. This helps to eliminate bulk while not decreasing the strength of the seam.

20. Take the lining panels and center twill tape over the waistline (on the right side of the fabric) and pin into place. Stitch along each edge of the twill tape to attach it to the right side of the corset lining. (You can stitch it to the wrong side so that the waist stay is hidden between the lining and shell, but this tends to affect the ability of the bones to slide easily into the casings – they snag on the waist stay edge). Your stitching lines will be seen only on the right side of the lining and not on the shell.

You have two separate panels, each with one side of a busk sewn in the middle, and raw edges at either end.

The raw edges are the center back. How you finish the center back will depend on if you're setting grommets or using lacing tape (See Section 2 Chapters 7 and 8). The steps here are preparing the center back for the setting of grommets. For details on the actual setting see Section 2 Chapter 7.

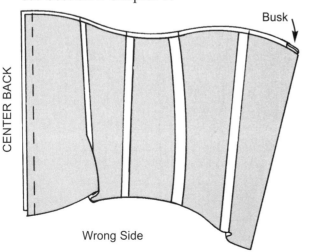

Wrong Side

21. The center backs need to be joined and finished. Turn the corset panels inside out and once you're sure that the raw edges are correctly aligned, stitch them using the seam allowance indicated on the pattern (right sides of lining and shell will be together). Press the stitched seam flat, then press it open and turn the corset right side out. Fold the center back seam into place and press again.

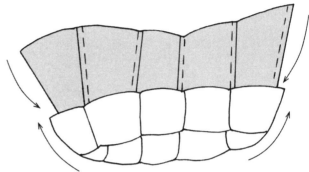

Turning corset right side out

22. Edgestitch the folded edge. Stitch a second row to create a bone casing parallel to the center back – the width of the casing will depend on the width of the bone you're using.

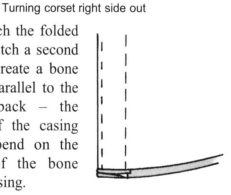

23. Before you sew any bone casings you need to recheck the fit of your layers. All of your seams have been pressed flat so your inside is neat and the shell and lining should fall into place as you lay each side on the table.

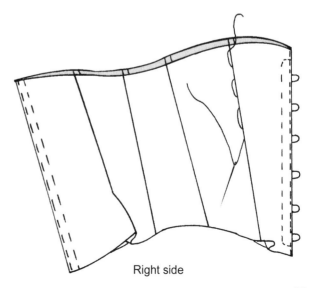

Right side

24. Line up all of your panels so that seams line up and top and bottom edges are parallel. Pin in place.

25. Hand stitch (baste) in the seams to attach both layers together. Your hand stitching should go through both the shell seam and the lining seam to stabilize their alignment. As tempting as it is to skip this step – *don't* as this keeps the two layers from shifting during the sewing of the bone casings.

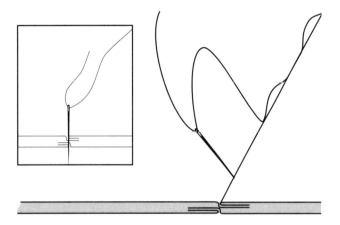

26. Machine stitch about ¼" (6mm) from the bottom edge of the corset. This will help keep your top and bottom edges lined up and stop the creeping that can occur when the casings are sewn.

27. Start machine stitching your bone casings on the outside of your corset by first stitching no more than ¹/₁₆" (1.5mm) from each seam edge, making the on-seam bone casings first. (A)

28. Stitch from bottom to top – on the outside of your corset. This is where sewing a straight line is important.

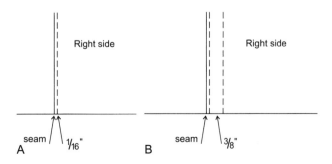

29. Stitch your second row of stitching to create the bone casings. (B) The width depends on the width of bones you're using. ³/₈" (9.5mm) is

good for ¼" (6mm) bones and acceptable for ⁵/₁₆" (8mm) bones – may be a bit tight though. The bone casings need to be snug enough to keep the bones from twisting within the casings.

30. Once you've completed all the on-seam bone casings flip the corset so that the lining side is up. You should be able to see your bone casing lines marked on the right side of the lining. You may have decided during the fitting of the mock-up that you need more bones and these lines should have been transferred to the lining by now. However you can still add some at this point if you need to.

31. Machine stitch these bone casing lines working from bottom to top.

32. You may want to remove the hand stitching from the seams, if it's visible.

33. Measure each bone casing to determine the length of bones you need and how many. You may have done this after fitting the mock-up. If so you'll have your bones ready and will just have to figure out which one goes in which casing. Lay your corset out flat with the right side facing the table and start laying the bones on top of the casings. Your bones should be the length of the casing from finished edge to finished edge less ½" (13mm). Purchased bones may be slightly longer or shorter but ½" (13mm) is the best difference in measurement. For more details on bones see Section 2 Chapters 2, 3, 4 and 5.

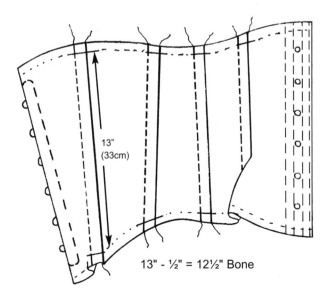

Note! Don't slide the bones in yet! If you do, slide them in to check the lengths, then remove them before finishing the bottom edge. It'll make the sewing easier if the bones are not in the corset. You may want to either label the bones or lay them on a table in order, so they can be easily picked up and inserted later.

34. Finish the bottom edge of the corset as directed in the pattern instructions. Usually this means binding the edge with bias tape. You may need to trim some bits depending on how well the pattern was drafted or how well you put it together. You're trimming to make a smooth raw edge.

35. Bind the edge as desired and described in Section 2 Chapter 11.

36. Slide your bones into the correct casings. Check that they're shorter than the casings. Push them down as far as they can go to get them out of the way so you can finish the top edge.

37. You'll need two lengths of fine cable cord or ribbon. The length depends on the length of the top edge, then add 10" (25cm). These two cords will be encased in the top edge of the corset and need to be long enough to get tied. Finish one end of each cord or ribbon so that they can't fray. Consider using lace tips as described in Section 2 Chapter 9. Anchor the opposite end to the top edge seam allowance near center back. (A)

38. Finish the top edge of the corset with bias tape, and be careful to keep the cable cord and the bones out of the way. The cable cord needs to be able to be moved through the bias tape casing, and hitting the bones with either the sewing machine foot or needle will be a problem. The finished ends of the cable cord or ribbon will come out the center front of the corset top edge and they can then be used as a draw-cord to adjust fit and increase security. (B)

Your Double Layer Corset is complete and ready to wear.

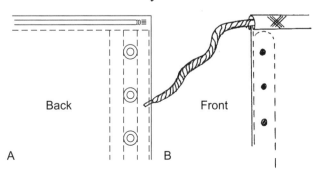

5. Building a Fashion Fabric Corset

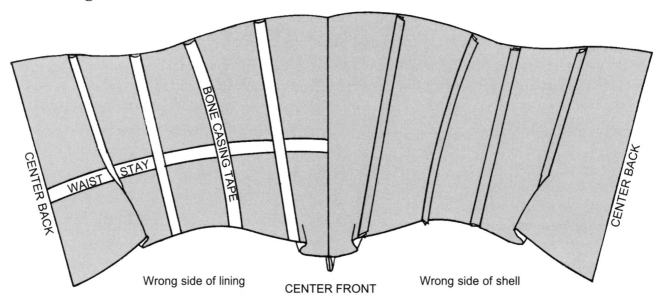

Wrong side of lining   CENTER FRONT   Wrong side of shell

To construct a fashion fabric corset you can follow the instructions in the previous chapters with a few variations. A fashion fabric corset must be built on a coutil base if it's to have the characteristics of a corset: support, shape and strength. Bones will wear holes in fashion fabric quickly and grommets will pop out easily. Considering the labor is the same regardless of the fabric used, it's better to build it right the first time and limit the need for repairs or irreparable damage. Use a coutil base no matter what your fashion fabric is – even if it's leather! Leather loves to stretch.

To make a fashion fabric corset based on single layer corset construction techniques you need to cut one layer of coutil and one layer of fashion fabric. Then combine some of the steps involved for both single and double layer corset construction.

1. Cut two layers of both coutil and fashion fabric. This will result in having a complete set of both left and right side corset panels and in both the shell (fashion fabric) and lining (coutil). *Don't* cut any facings.

2. Before removing the pattern pieces from your fabric label each and *every* piece in the top corner within the seam allowance. Keep the labeling simple but be sure not to omit this step as it's very easy to get the pieces mixed

up and even sewn on upside down! Label them in the order they go together as this is the whole point of labeling – keeping construction simple. You can start with 1, 2, 3, etc., or use dots. This was discussed in detail in Section 2 Chapter 1.

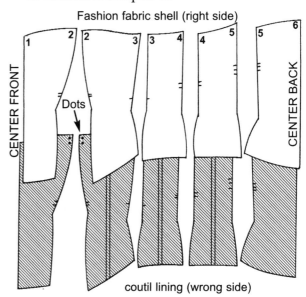

Fashion fabric shell (right side)

coutil lining (wrong side)
Illustration represents left side of corset only.

3. Mark your bone casings on the wrong side of the lining (coutil) pieces. This means the bone casing markings will be on the side of the coutil that faces the fashion fabric and is between the lining and the shell. You can mark the casing on the right side of the lining, but this means the bone casing is against your body.

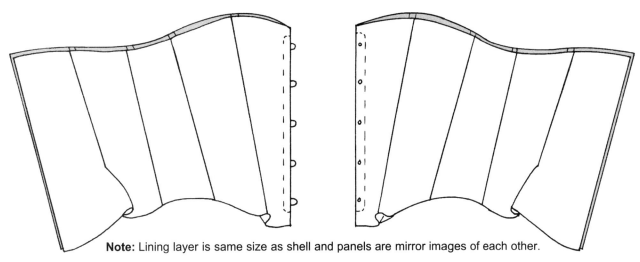

Note: Lining layer is same size as shell and panels are mirror images of each other.

Note: If your shell (fashion fabric) is delicate or light the casings may cause unattractive ridges when sewn on the wrong side of the lining. You may want to test a small scrap of bone casing with your fashion fabric before deciding where you'll sew the casings.

4. Lay out the pieces in order on the table. Lay each pattern piece side by side in the order they'll be sewn. You'll have all of your left side pattern pieces, and all of your right side pieces, and there will be your labels in each top corner.

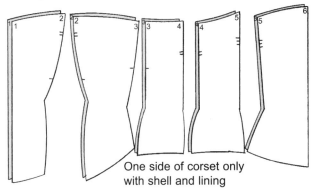

One side of corset only with shell and lining

5. You can now apply the busk as described in Section 2 Chapter 6 using all four front pieces. The front lining pieces will be treated like facings and the front fashion fabric pieces are the shell. I recommend that you apply a fusible interfacing to your front and back shell pieces. This will help stabilize them and limit problems of fraying when you punch holes for grommets in the back or force holes with an awl in the front. Choose a fusible interfacing that suits your fashion fabric.

6. Sew your lining (coutil) pieces together and fashion fabric (shell) pieces together in the labeled order – creating two panels, being sure that no piece gets sewn on upside down. It sounds easy enough but I've seen many errors in sewing the pieces together. The pieces are almost impossible to identify and you may not discover you made a mistake until you try to fit the corset, so watch the labels!

Note: You'll end up with only two panels each with a busk in the middle. *See illustration above.*

7. Once the sewing is complete lay the corset out to assure yourself all the pieces are in the right order. The two panels should be mirror images of each other.

    If they aren't then you have to take your pattern pieces and lay them on top of the corset to discover where you went wrong and then unpick the seam. Watch your labels to avoid this problem. When you lay the pieces on top of one another, as they'll eventually be sewn, check that they fit – that the lining is the same size as the shell. If there is a discrepancy fix it before you go any further.

8. Sew each of your seams a second time using a different length stitch. This will strengthen the seam and will be less likely to rip like a perforated stamp. Consider 8 stitches per inch and 12 stitches per inch.

9. Press all your seams. All lining seams get pressed toward center front and all shell

seams get pressed toward center back. This helps to eliminate bulk while not decreasing the strength of the seam.

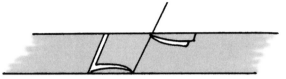

Visible Bone Casings (does not have waist stay)
Skip to step #12

10. Take the lining panels and center twill tape over the waistline (on the wrong side of the lining) and pin it into place. Stitch along each edge of the twill tape to attach it to the wrong side of the corset lining. Your stitching lines will be seen only on the right side of the lining and not on the shell. The twill tape waist stay could bc scwn on the right side of the fabric but the chances of rough spots chafing the skin are less when it's sewn to the wrong side, away from the skin.

Invisible bone casings
Continue with step #11

11. Apply bone casing tape to the wrong side of the lining. Begin with the on-seam bone casings. Line up the bone casing with the seam stitching and sew by machine, first along the side closest to the seam and then along the side covering the raw edge. You'll be sewing the casings over the waist stay. Stitching will only be seen on the right side of the lining.

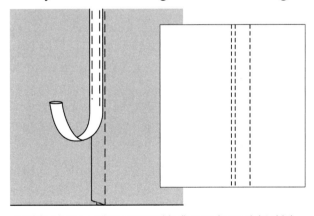

Applying bone casing, wrong side (insert shows right side)

12. Pin your bone casing tapes onto your lining (coutil) pieces as indicated by the lines you traced onto the fabric pieces. Take one piece

at a time (helps keep the pieces organized) to the sewing machine and stitch your casings to the fabric. Stitch along both edges using the grooves on each side of the casing tape as a guide. Don't stitch into the channel as this could affect your bone being able to slide in.

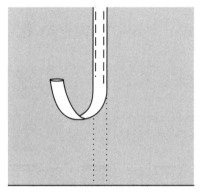

Bone casing being used for mid-piece or non-on-seam casings, for both visible and invisible methods.

13. Turn the corset panels wrong side out and line up the center back raw edges. Stitch them using the seam allowance indicated on the pattern.

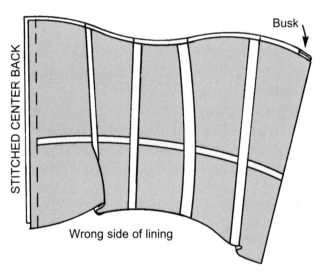

Busk

STITCHED CENTER BACK

Wrong side of lining

14. Press the stitched seam flat, then press it open and turn the corset right side out. Fold the center back seam into place and press again.

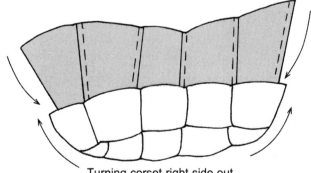

Turning corset right side out

15. Edge stitch the folded edge. Stitch a second row to create a bone casing along the center back – the width of the casing will depend on the width of the bone you're using.

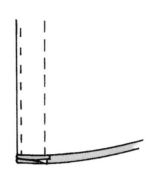

16. Before you go any further recheck the fit of your layers. All of your seams have been pressed flat so your inside is neat and the shell and lining should fall into place as you lay each side on the table.

17. Line up all of your pieces so that seams line up and so do top and bottom edges. Pin in place.

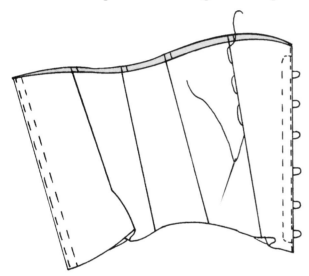

18. Hand stitch in the seams to attach both layers together. Your hand stitching shouldn't be visible and should go through both the shell seam and the lining seam to stabi-

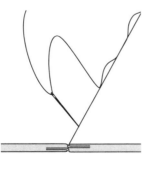

lize their alignment. As tempting as it is to skip this step – *don't* as this keeps the two layers from shifting during the completion of the corset, particularily if you are now going to sew visible bone casings.

19. Machine stitch about ¼" (6mm) from the bottom edge of the corset. This will help keep your top and bottom edges lined up and stop the creeping that can occur when the visible bone casings are sewn.

Visible Bone Casings
Continue with step #20

Invisible bone casings
Skip to step #23.

20. Start machine stitching your bone casings on the outside of your corset by first stitching no more than ¹/₁₆" (1.5mm) from each seam edge, stitching from bottom to top, (A) making the on seam bone casings through the fashion fabric and the lining seam allowances. The bones will be slid between the two layers of lining seam allowance leaving a layer of coutil and a layer of fashion fabric between the bone and the outside world and two layers of coutil between the bone and the wearer's body.

This is where stitching a straight line is important.

Stitch your second row of stitching to create the bone casings. The width depends on the width of bones you're using. ³/₈" (9.5mm) is good for ¼" (6mm) bones and acceptable for ⁵/₁₆" (8mm) bones – but may be a bit tight. The bone casings need to be snug enough to keep the bones from twisting within the casings. (B)

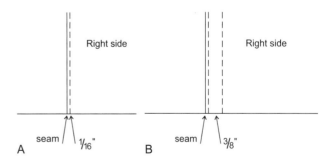

21. Once you've completed all the on-seam bone casings flip the corset so that the lining side is up. You should be able to see your bone casing lines as they've already been stitched to the lining. You may have decided during the fitting of the mock-up that you need more

bones and bone casing should have been added before now.

22. Machine stitch these bone casing lines working from bottom to top stitching over the original stitch lines that attached the bone casings to the lining on the wrong side.

    This makes your casing visible on the outside while your bones are still securely encased in bone casing tape.

23. You may want to remove the hand basting from the seams, if it's visible.

24. Measure each bone casing to determine the length of bones you need and how many. You may have done this after fitting the mock-up. If so you'll have your bones ready and will just have to figure out which one goes in which casing. Lay your corset out flat with the right side facing the table and start laying the bones on top of the casings. Your bones should be the length of the casing from finished edge to finished edge less ½" (13mm). Purchased bones maybe slightly longer or slightly shorter but ½" (13mm) is the best difference in measurement. For more details on bones see Section 2 Chapters 2, 3, 4 and 5.

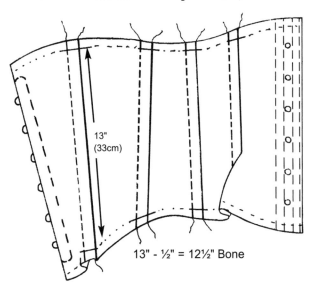

13" (33cm)

13" - ½" = 12½" Bone

Note: Don't slide the bones in yet! If you do slide them in to check the lengths then remove them before finishing the bottom edge. It'll make the sewing easier if the bones aren't in the corset. You may want to either label the bones or lay them on a table in order, so they can be easily picked up and inserted later.

25. Finish the bottom edge of the corset as directed in the pattern instructions. Usually this means binding the edge with bias tape – make bias tape from your fashion fabric. You may need to trim some bits along the bottom depending on how well the pattern was drafted or how well you put it together. You're trimming to make a smooth raw edge. For instructions on binding the edges see Section 2 Chapter 11.

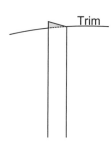

Trim

26. Slide your bones into the correct casings. Check they're shorter than the casings. Push them down as far as they can go to get them out of the way so you can finish the top edge.

27. You'll need two lengths of fine cable cord or ribbon. The length depends on the length of the top edge, then add 10" (25cm). These two cords will be encased in the top edge of the corset and need to be long enough to get tied. Finish one end of each cord or ribbon so that they can't fray. Consider using lace tips as described in Section 2 Chapter 9. Anchor the opposite end to the top edge seam allowance near center back. (A)

28. Finish the top edge of the corset with bias tape cut from the fashion fabric (see Section 2 Chapter 11 for details). Be careful to keep the cable cord/ribbon and the bones out of the way. The cable cord needs to be able to be moved through the bias tape casing, and hitting the bones with either the sewing machine foot or needle will be a problem. The finished ends of the cable cord or ribbon will come out the center front of the corset top edge and can then be used as a drawcord to fine-tune the fit. (B)

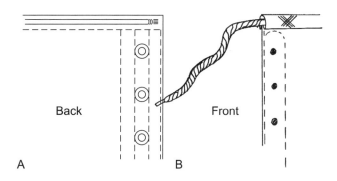

Back   Front

A   B

Your Fashion Fabric Corset is complete and ready to wear.

Section Four: Pattern Alterations and Fit

1. Commercial Corset Patterns

There are a surprising number of period corset patterns available today *but* they're not all created equal. I recommend Laughing Moon Mercantile's Dore corset pattern and Simplicity's #9769 as both of these patterns are simple to construct, fit and restyle, and both are professionally drafted and come with fairly extensive instructions. For those concerned with historic authenticity both of these patterns were drafted based on museum pieces from the 1800s.

Laughing Moon Dore Corset

The Laughing Moon pattern is made by a small pattern company in California owned by a woman whose primary focus of research is the late Victorian era. The Laughing Moon pattern isn't sold through chain stores but can be found online from several sources. It contains two different corset patterns – the Silverado and the Dore – and the size range within one pattern envelope is 6 – 26 (bust 30½" or 78cm to 48" or roughly 123cm). I suggest starting with the Dore corset as the Silverado has bust gores and for some people this is a new detail. The instructions for the Dore corset are for a double layer corset and the instructions are extensive and easy to follow. The pattern is well drafted and all pieces fit perfectly.

Simplicity Corset #9769

You'll likely recognize the name Simplicity, a pattern company based in the USA but selling patterns through retail chains all over the world. Not all countries sell all the same patterns so this pattern may not be available in your area but you may find it online. It was drafted by a costume

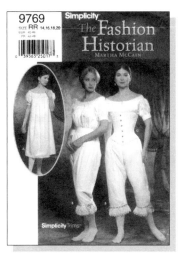

historian, and like the Laughing Moon one, is based on historical research so you get not only a great contemporary look, but also know your corset is appropriate to the time periods stated. This pattern comes in two size groups; size 6 – 12 [bust 30½" (78cm) to 34" (86cm)] and size 14 – 20 [bust 36" (91.5cm) to 42" inch (107cm)]. The instructions that come with this pattern are for a single layer corset. Simplicity does have another corset pattern but it doesn't lend itself easily to fitting so I don't recommend it for the beginner. Simplicity does occasionally discontinue patterns but I hope this one will be available for a while.

Now, to discuss in general terms the patterns that I haven't recommended here. There are many out there and some are decent, but the ones mentioned are the best and most straightforward to use. There are things to look for when considering other patterns and you'll only find out these details by asking other users. So you may want to get on a chat group or web site that critiques historic patterns.

Is the pattern an exact reproduction of an original?
Sounds cool but beware.

- The pattern may not come with instructions.
- There may be missing pieces.
- The size likely wouldn't fit you, and may not be anywhere near fitting you. (Remember people were smaller 150 years ago and they had spent their lives corseted.)

Was the pattern professionally drafted?
This is important; there are many people who can draft a pattern but not draft it well. A pattern that isn't drafted well will have pieces that don't fit

together properly and this can be frustrating. It also means that the garment may not fit well and you'll be left with a lot of fiddling to get the garment made.

Has the pattern been graded to various sizes?
If the answer is *No* then you know the pattern will have to be graded up or down before you can even cut the mock-up. If you don't have grading skills or don't know what grading is – don't buy the pattern.

Are there good instructions?
This is really important and a common weakness of historic patterns. Once you've read this book and built a corset or two, the instructions with a corset pattern won't be so important – but they'll be important for other garments.

2. Fitting a Corset

A whole book could be written on fitting corsets as there are many cuts and even more body types. It's impossible to cover the fitting process of all of them here so only a few more common issues will be covered. The basic principles can be applied to most bodies and many corset patterns, but not to all. *Be aware that you'll need more than one fitting!* This is likely the most fitted garment you've ever made and there should be no ease. Fitting needs to be accurate for the corset to be comfortable. And don't be afraid of the alteration process. It'll make more sense when you see the corset on the body and start exploring all the possible alteration potential that the many seams offer you.

- 1st fitting – mock-up, no bones or busk – check circumference.
- 2nd fitting – mock-up with bones, no busk – check length, confirm circumference.
- 3rd fitting – good fabric with bones and busk – confirm the fit is right.
- 4th fitting – the completed corset.

The fitting sample used here is a classic Victorian five panel corset (five panels on each side of the body for a total of ten panels around the body) common both during the American Civil War and later. It's an easy corset to build and to alter and is a great first corset project. Commercial patterns for this style of corset are available from Simplicity and Laughing Moon Mercantile. You can find more information on both in the previous chapter.

Note: *Always* read *all* instructions before cutting!

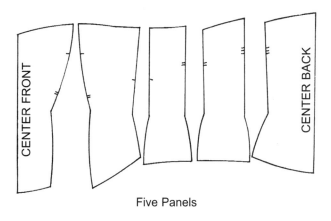

Five Panels

Always cut your corset out of scrap fabric and make a mock-up first, before cutting your coutil which is fairly expensive fabric. You'll need someone to assist you in the fitting if you're making the corset for yourself. Decide how you'll fit the mock-up before cutting the pieces out. If you have lacing tape you can baste it to the center backs or, if you don't, you'll need to add 2" or 50.8 cm to each center back so that the gap designed into the fit won't exist, and you'll be able to pin the back shut for fitting. Information for using lacing tape can be found in Section 2 Chapter 8.

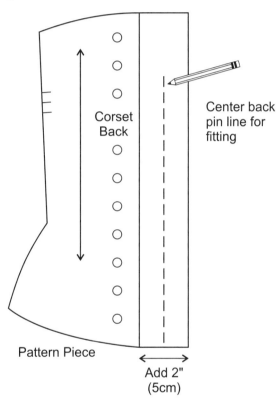

Extension, marking the new center back

To fit the corset properly you need to be almost naked. Wear only underwear and particularly a bra that offers similar support to that which you want the corset to offer. For modesty's sake you could wear a thin nylon slip but nothing loose or bulky.

Never make alteration marks to only one side of a corset and assume that they'll be correct for both sides. Patterns tend to be symmetrical but bodies aren't and this is particularly evident when fitting a corset. Always mark both sides of the corset while it's on the body

Have pins, a seam ripper, extra scrap fabric, scissors, and a marking pen handy for the fitting. You may be marking the alterations on the fabric and that's why you need to make a mock-up. Read *all* of these instructions before you cut your good fabric.

Have an assistant lace or pin you into the corset, depending on which method you chose. *It's easier if the seam allowances are on the outside not facing your body.*

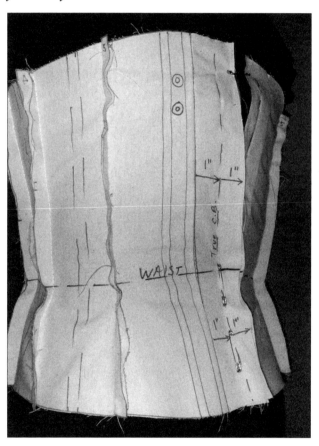

Note that the center back seam does not meet all the way up. The corset is too small in the chest circumference.

Note: This means that your mock-up will be the equivalent to your lining and so you have to be very careful when cutting your shell and keep the left side alterations on the left side of the body. This will be discussed in detail later but be sure to think about this fact. You'll get better results if you have an experienced assistant; if you know someone else who is building a corset, you can fit each other.

First Fitting – wearing a good support bra and panties

Check the basic fit of the corset.

- Does it fit around the body?
- Does it ride up anywhere and wrinkle?
- Does it come high enough on the bust? Too high?
- Does it fit around the tummy?
- Does the center front seam remain vertical or does it slant?

Note: If you've cut your corset out based on your measurements as they related to the corset size measurements you may have few if any alterations. But you may also find that you have to take some seams in and let others out, depending on where your fullness is – or isn't. It isn't uncommon to have to apply both types of alteration techniques on one corset.

Letting the corset out

1. No matter how much or how little you need to let the corset out you'll need to unpick a seam or two. This is easiest using a seam ripper and gently picking or cutting each stitch while the corset is on the body.

   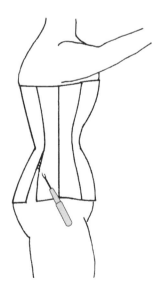

   Only open that part of the seam that needs to be adjusted. Don't open the whole seam.

2. You may only need to readjust the seam allowance. If so pin the seam allowance where it now needs to be and mark the new stitching line with your pen on both pieces of fabric. *Don't use disappearing ink!*

3. You may need to let the seam out more than the seam allowance can accommodate. In this case you'll need extra scrap fabric and scissors to cut a patch. Cut one roughly the size and shape you need – it's only a mock-up so it doesn't need to be accurate, but it does need to be bigger than the gap.

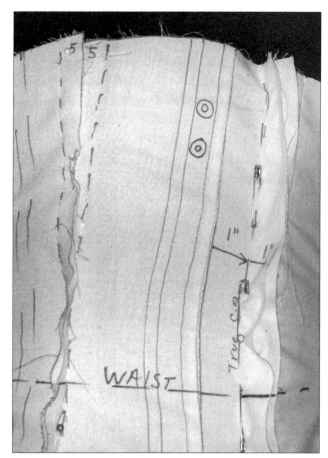

This seam has been opened and let out until the center back seam could close.

4. Pin the patch into place and mark the stitching line on the patch.

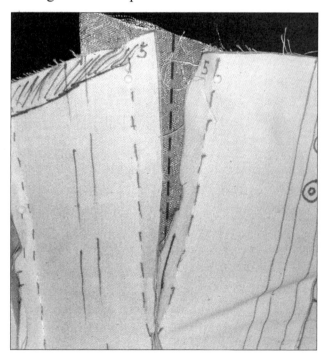

5. Do this for all seams that require it.

Taking the Corset in

1. To take in a seam don't rip it out. Simply pinch the extra seam allowance and pin it.

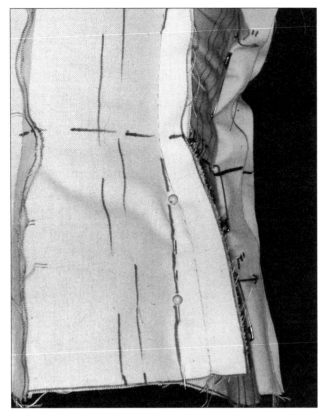

Note original stitched seam, pinned and marked new seam.

2. Mark the new stitching line onto the mock-up with your pen.

3. Do this for all seams that require it.

Making the Adjustments

- The seams that get taken in are easy to change on the mock-up by simply machine basting the new seam lines.
- The seams that have been let out only a small amount are also easy to machine baste along the new stitching line.
- The seams that have required a patch need to have the patch machine sewn onto the mock-up so they can't shift. The seam line is drawn onto the patch.
- All alterations noted in the first fitting should be sewn for the second fitting.

Preparing for the Second Fitting – (no bra this time)

1. Baste the bone casing tape or twill tape (use anything just to create bone channels) into place over marked bone casing lines but not on the seams. Press seam allowances to one side and baste to the corset. Use this as you sew on the on-seam bone casings – if needed.

2. Slide bones into the casings.

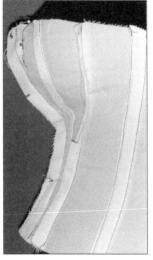 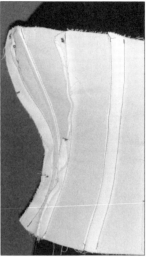

Before bones   After Bones

3. Try on the corset as before; this time you won't be wearing a bra as the bones are now in the corset to offer support. Check to see if they're doing the job.

4. Check the fit. Are the alterations you made solving the problems? Are the bones supporting the body? Keep in mind there will be a few more bones in the seams and these will help a bit – but you may decide to add more bones. Decide this now.

5. Baste on more bone casings if you want to and test the fit again. Placement of the bones can follow the direction of the original casings or you may need support at a different angle – every body is different and you can place the bones where you need them.

6. Be sure to move around and sit down in your corset during the fitting with bones. Note if they poke into you anywhere – the most common places are under the arms, into the shoulder blades, hips, and into the pubic bone when sitting down.

7. If they're poking in anywhere then the corset is too long at that spot. This is why I suggest plastic bones for beginners as they are easy to cut down.

8. Remove the corset from your body. If you've laced it then unlace it completely before taking it off so that you don't disturb any of the pins.

9. You now have to transfer your changes to your pattern. This is easiest if you carefully rip out all the basted seams after first securing all the pinned-on pieces and cutting any patches along the stitching line.

10. You have a choice: you can use your mock-up as a new pattern, but if you do you need to add seam allowance wherever your seam allowance diminished. *Or* you can cut out another copy of your pattern but you must have a left and a right side of all corset pieces. It's imperative to have a left and a right side as your body isn't symmetrical and your alterations are side specific.

11. Create the new pattern and label every piece as outlined previously. Now add an L or an R for left and right.

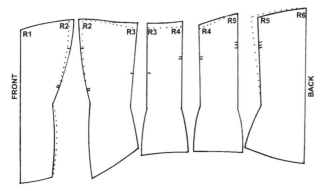

12. Check that the pattern alterations are where they should be – on the correct side of the body. Check all seam allowances to confirm they're all the same.

13. If you're confident then cut the new pattern out of good fabric. Use the lining layer if you're doing a two layer corset, just in case.

14. Baste the seams together, including center front but not center back.

Shortening and Lengthening the Corset

You can do this during your original fitting before you have casing and boning, but you won't get an accurate feel for the length so it's better to do this in the second fitting. You need to have let out or taken in the seams first as the fit in circumference will affect the fit in length. If the corset is too tight and rides up causing waist wrinkles then you won't see the actual finished length. Shortening and lengthening can also be used for altering the look or style of your corset.

Note: You'll need an assistant with this fitting process.

Shortening

The corset seams have been adjusted so that the corset fits you, and casings are basted on with bones in them so you can get an accurate idea of the length of the corset. You have the corset on and notice that bones are poking you. You'll be able to feel where the corset needs to be shortened and your assistant needs to mark these points with your marking pen.

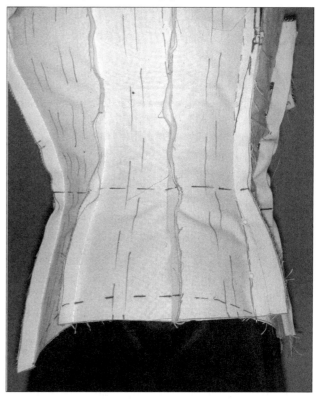

1. After the shortened points are marked you need to connect the dots by drawing a smooth line, blending to the original finished edge if needed. It's best to do this while the corset is still on the body as you'll get a better idea of the finished look.

2. The line you're drawing is the finished edge. When you transfer the marking to your pattern you'll need to add seam allowance.

Lengthening

1. You'll need scraps of mock-up fabric if you find you need to lengthen the corset anywhere. Determine where you want to lengthen it and pin a piece of scrap fabric to the corset.

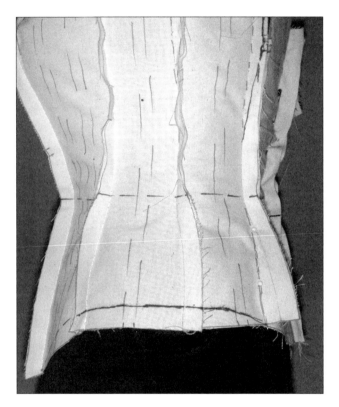

2. Since your scrap is flat you may have to pin some shape into it so that it follows the line of the body closely.

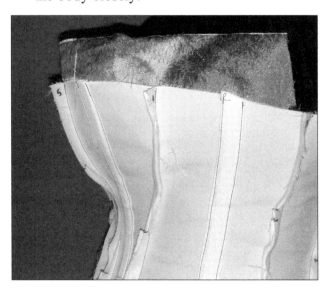

3. Mark the new length on the scrap fabric with a marking pen.

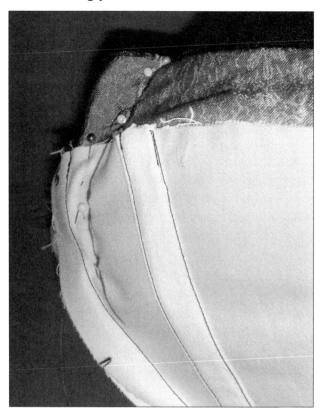

4. Connect the dots with a smooth line; blend into the original if needed.

5. This is your finished edge and will need seam allowance added when you transfer this marking to the pattern.

There are many areas that may need to be lengthened or shortened depending on your body. The above techniques can be applied to most of them.

Body Challenges

Many people have a curvature to their spine and this will seriously affect the fit of a corset. If the fit isn't adjusted the corset won't only be uncomfortable but won't look right as the horizontal lines of the top and bottom edges will tilt. One breast may be covered and the other exposed. Visually you want the top and bottom edges to be parallel to the ground and the busk to be vertical, not tilted. This is particularly important if the corset is for outerwear as in an evening or bridal bodice. In this instance you may find you have to add to the top edge on one side and take away on the other. It's very important to always know what side of the body you're working with so be sure to always label your pieces, not only with sequential numbers but with right and left side. This can get very confusing even with labeling so test fit the final garment in a basted state to confirm you have the right and left sides where they need to be.

It may seem like a waste of time but trying to unpick a complete corset takes even longer.

The illustration shows a straight easy-to-fit body and the effects of a curved spine. The dashed line indicates a line parallel to the floor and the dotted lines indicate possible alterations (the alterations shown here are just to suggest what to consider).

Challenges to fitting for a curved spine – front view

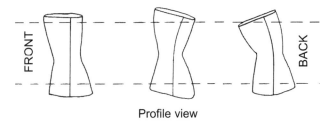

FRONT   BACK

Profile view

There is a lot involved in fitting a curved spine but if you start with a mock-up you'll have the opportunity to discover and solve the problems at minimal cost. Imagine discovering that one breast was exposed after you had cut the good fabric!

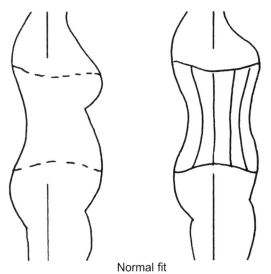

Normal fit

Other fitting challenges include someone whose spine tips backwards, has developed a hunch, or has a large tummy. The corset may fit all of these individuals in circumference but not in the right places. You may need to alter the top and bottom edges to make them parallel to the ground, and you'll likely need to take some seams in while letting others out – yet still end up with the same circumference measurement.

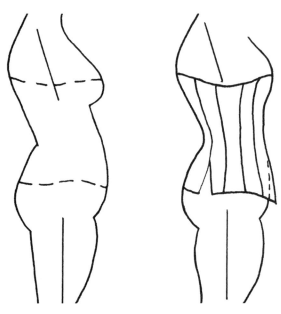

A tipped body with poorly fit corset having to let out a side seam and take in the front seam – profile view

The tipped spine means that when looking at the profile the pelvis seems to be ahead of the chest. This will affect the seam lines as the whole corset will appear to tilt with the body especially if seams are detailed with piping. A corset can be the right size or even a bit big and not fit the tilted body well.

This type of alteration may require you to re-cut the pattern pieces depending on the severity of the tilt. Depending on the corset pattern you want the side seams to be more or less vertical, but if they are not dead-on vertical don't worry.

What is important is that all panels are cut following the grain lines drawn on the pattern pieces, as the grain lines have been drawn so that the panels will have the least likelihood of stretching which increases the strength of the corset.

The hunched body tends to create a concave area below the chest, and contrary to popular belief, a

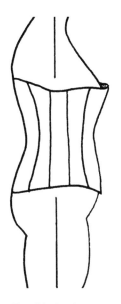 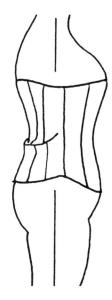

Too big in chest   Too small over bum

corset won't help your hunched posture unless it comes up high over your shoulder blades. I won't be covering that fitting challenge here. The focus of fit for someone who is hunched will be on the chest area as the average Victorian corset doesn't come above the shoulder blades. To properly fit a corset on this person, it's best to have the bones in the mock-up from the beginning as their breasts will need to be raised.

There are many challenges to fitting a corset, so approach fitting with patience and time – don't rush. All fitting challenges can be conquered by applying the techniques described here.

Hint: Cut 1" seam allowances when you cut the mock-up

3. Styling a Corset

To style a corset can mean many things. It may mean something as simple as adding lace and ribbon or as complex as changing the cut of the corset. Below are some samples of what can be done and some hints on how these styles were accomplished. You can make the same pattern out of various fabrics and get very different looks. This is the easiest way to create a unique corset. All six of these corsets were made using the Laughing Moon Dore pattern or Simplicity 9769. By simply using different fabrics the whole image changes!

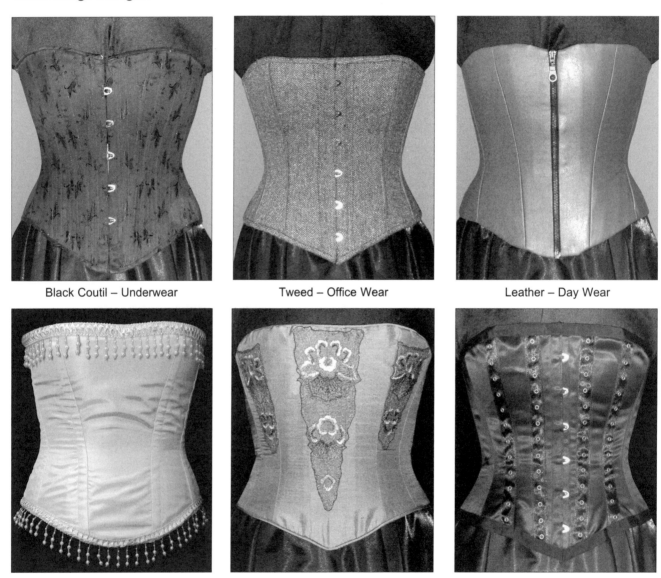

| Black Coutil – Underwear | Tweed – Office Wear | Leather – Day Wear |
| Pink Taffeta | Green Silk with Appliqués | Touch of Gothic |

The black coutil corset is a double layer corset and the bone casings are visible on the outside. The tweed and leather corsets are single layer construction corsets with a single layer of coutil, bone casing tape, and a single layer of fashion fabric. There are no bone casings showing on the outside of these corsets. The brown leather corset has a heavy zipper at center front rather than a busk and works well with jeans. The tweed corset would of course be worn over a blouse and likely with a matching skirt. Corsets can be anything!

Note: If using a zipper it must be heavy and it must be separating. Most importantly you have to loosen the back lacing to remove any tension on the zipper as it's being done up, or you'll pop teeth off the zipper and have to replace the whole thing. Once the zipper is done up you can tighten the lacing with little worry.

Embelishing can also be a simple way to personalize your corset and this was quite common historically. Depending on your handiwork skills you may want to embroider the corset panels or sew on appliqués. Or, you may add patchwork panels, grommets for decoration, pipe the seams, or paint designs on the corset. Consider the corset a blank canvas!

The *Pink Taffeta* corset has been made without a front opening busk to create a more traditional strapless bodice look. Otherwise, the pattern hasn't been altered in any way. Finishing touches include matching rayon braid and crystal beaded drops along the top and bottom edges. Pink ribbon laces up the back over a modesty panel.

The *Green Silk* corset with appliqués was also made without a front opening busk. Vintage appliqués were sewn onto the silk outer layer before it was attached to the coutil foundation. The top and bottom edges were finished with matching piping cord rather than bound with bias, and the grommets in the back are antique brass to complete the outerwear look.

The *Touch of Gothic* corset is a single layer corset made with black satin coutil. Decorative satin ribbon preset with nickel eyelets has been used over a few of the bone casings, further defining style lines. The top and bottom edges were finished with petersham.

Note: Attachment of appliqués was done prior to putting the corsets together. It can be done after but only if you can avoid stitching through any bone casings.

Changing the placement of the lacing from the back to the front or sides will also change the look of your corset without much challenge. This corset laces up in front as well as in back. The front lacing is both a design feature and functional as it allows the wearer to get into the corset by themselves. The back lacing provides the fit adjustment necessary with such a fitted garment.

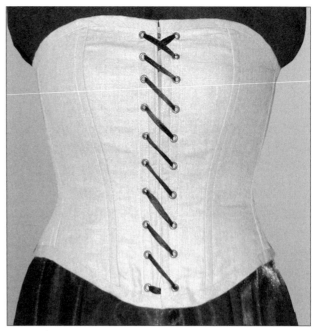

Note: To get into this corset you have to completely undo the front lace, wrap the corset around your body, hold it on by pressing your elbows to your sides, and relace the front. This isn't a quick process! Also, if lacing up the front you may want to include a modesty panel. A simple rectangular panel made from your fashion fabric can be hand sewn to the inside of the corset to fill in any gap. This means if there is a space between the two center fronts no skin will be visible. You can use this same idea for the back of your corset. For more information see Section 3 Chapter 1. Changing the lacing pattern changes the look.

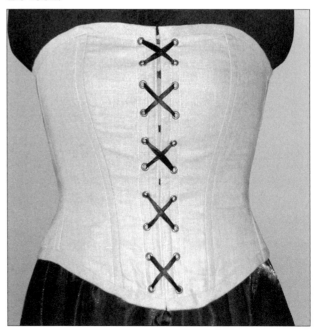

Section Four: Pattern Alterations and Fit

If you're a bit more adventurous you may want to reshape your top or bottom edge as well. All of the drawings below are based on the same basic corset shape. They've each simply had the top and bottom edges reshaped. This isn't a difficult alteration but it's most easily accomplished by making a mock-up first and adding fabric where needed. It's best not to attempt this until you have made the pattern as designed first.

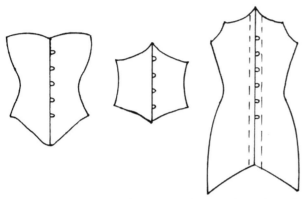

All of the corsets above can be made using the Laughing Moon Mercantile – Dore corset pattern. The one on the left is from an unaltered pattern, the one in the middle has had the top and bottom edges altered, and the one on the right has been changed dramatically.

Glossary

A

aglets – small steel tips applied with aglet pliers to cord ends to keep them from fraying.

awl – a small metal spike with a handle used for making holes in your fabric.

B

baste – stitch loosely together in preparation for sewing.

bias – diagonal line or cut across the weave of a fabric.

bias tape (strip) – a strip of fabric that is cut on the bias of a fabric rather than with or across the grain, used to bind the top and bottom edges of corsets to finish them.

bodice – a woman's sleeveless garment, usually laced in the front, and worn over a blouse or dress; the part of a woman's dress or blouse which is above the waist.

bolt cutters – tool for cutting steel bones.

bones – the support for the corset.

broadcloth – a closely woven fabric of wool, cotton, silk, or a mixture of the three; a densely woven woollen cloth in a plain or twill weave and having a lustrous finish.

brocade – a rich fabric with a silky finish woven with a raised pattern, and often with gold or silver thread.

busk – a strip of wood, whalebone, steel, etc., used for stiffening the front of a corset.

busk knob – the clasp that closes the center front.

C

cable cord – used within the top edge of the corset and encased in the bias binding.

casings (bone casings) – a flattened tube of material to keep the bones in position and help decrease the potential for holes developing in the corset as the bones shift during wearing.

coutil – a durable corseting fabric specifically designed for use in building corsets.

D

double cord lacing – using two separate cords to lace up the corset, as opposed to just one.

doublet – a man's short close-fitting jacket, either with or without sleeves.

double-wheel tracing wheel – tracing wheel with two wheels that create parallel lines; can be adjusted to different distances apart in order to create markings for various sizes of bones.

drawcord – draws in the top edge of the corset for added security.

E

edge stitching – keeps lining or facing from twisting around the bone and busk.

eyelet – see grommet.

F

fusible interfacing – helps stabilize the fabric and removes the possibility of fraying around the grommet holes.

G

grommet – a round metal or plastic two-piece reinforcement placed in the hole to hold the lacing in place. It should be supported on either side by a spring steel bone unless a lacing bone is being used.

H

hand-sewing needles – thinner needles used to sew garments by hand, as opposed to sewing machine needles.

herringbone – a weave with a zig-zag pattern resembling the bones of a herring.

L

lace tips – tips made of either steel or plastic to keep cord ends from fraying.

lacing bone – a flat steel bone with holes punched into it, evenly spaced and designed to fit grommets or eyelets.

lacing cord – closes the back and adjusts the fit of the corset.

lacing tape – a fabric tape with eyelets already preset on it.

M

millinery – the art of making women's hats.

modesty panel (placket) – found behind the lacing down the center back and is made out of matching exterior fabric. It's used for two reasons: to hide the flesh which would otherwise be visible behind the lacing, and to protect the skin from abrasion that could be caused by the laces.

N

needle-nose pliers – pliers having long, thin pincers suitable for gripping in very narrow spaces.

P

petersham ribbon – can be used in place of bias tape for finishing the top and bottom edges of a corset by binding them.

R

rotary cutter – a small wheel-shaped blade with a handle used to cut fabric on a cutting mat.

rubber mallet – used with hole punches or for setting grommets or eyelets in the back of your corset.

S

seam allowance – amount of material along each edge of the piece of a garment which is taken in by a seam.

selvedge – an edging that prevents cloth from fraying; either an edge along the warp or a specially woven edging.

shrink tips – small clear tubes that can be melted with the heat of a lit candle, hair drier or iron, that create the same look you'll find on most shoelaces.

single cord lacing – one end is anchored to the corset and the other end threads through the grommets/eyelets.

spiral steels – type of bone that flexes from side to side as well as from front to back. Looks like a coil of wire that has been stretched slightly and then flattened.

spring steels – type of bone that flexes only from front to back and used also for the centre back of all corsets to help support the grommets or eyelets used for lacing.

stays/steels – see bone.

T

thimble – cap of metal or plastic worn on the end of the finger to protect it while sewing.

thread snips – small tool used to trim thread.

tight lacing – when a corset is worn regularly, day and night, and pulled to get the smallest waist possible. This puts a great strain on the corset.

tin snips – a pair of hand-held shears used to cut metal.

tracing wheel – tool used to trace a pattern onto fabric by use of a small wheel with points, attached to a handle, run over tracing paper.

twill tape – tape made of a woven fabric with a surface of diagonal parallel ridges, used to finish an edge.

U

"U" tips – small U-shaped aluminium or steel pieces which fit onto the ends of various steel bones. They blunt the ends and inhibit them from creating holes in the fabric when the rough ends rub against the fabric during wear.

W

waist stay – twill tape or petersham ribbon sewn into the corset waist area for extra support.

For more information about the products discussed in this book, visit **www.farthingales.on.ca**

About the Author:

Linda Sparks was born in Toronto, Ontario, and graduated from George Brown College with a degree in fashion. Her career started in the Toronto fashion industry, but a move to the country changed her direction and she began costume building for the Stratford Festival Theatre in the late 1980s.

After almost ten years in theater, she opened Farthingales in 1997, a company she created to supply architectural products to the theater industry of North America. Farthingales stocks unique products like corset making materials that can't be found in most fabric stores.

In 2006 Linda opened Farthingales L.A. Inc. to better supply the US market. Farthingales L.A. Inc. is a corset shop, selling the raw materials, patterns, books and both ready-made corsets and custom corsets. The L.A. location is also where Linda teaches her corset-making workshops.

www.farthingalesLA.com (ships only within the USA)
www.farthingales.on.ca (ships all over the world)